mayakovsky
russian poet

a memoir
by
elsa triolet
1939

Translated by Susan de Muth 2002

HEARING EYE

First published 2002
HEARING EYE
Box 1, 99 Torriano Avenue, NW5 2RX

Translation © Susan de Muth 2002
Translation introduction © Susan de Muth 2002

With thanks to the original copyright holder Jean Ristat.

The publication of this volume was assisted by London Arts

ISBN 1 870841 83 2

Printed in Britain by Sherlock Printing, Bolney, West Sussex

ACKNOWLEDGEMENTS

I am extremely grateful to Irina Padva and Dr Paulina Chernilovskaya for their skill and tireless patience in interpreting Mayakovsky's verse to me. The new translations of extracts fom his poetic works which appear in this volume would not have been possible without them.

The website www.mayakovsky.com also proved an invaluable research tool.

Many thanks also to Susan Johns for her help in preparing this book.

CONTENTS

Introduction by Susan de Muth   **5**

Mayakovsky, Russian Poet   **by Elsa Triolet**

Preface	**9**
Chapter 1	**12**
2	31
3	49
4	56
5	66
6	85
Translator's notes	**95**
Bibliography	**102**

INTRODUCTION

Mayakovsky, Russian Poet - a Memoir is a unique insight into the life and works of one of the most important artists of the 20th century. Elsa Triolet (1896 - 1970) was on intimate terms with Mayakovsky for 18 years and knew him variously as lover, friend, poet and champion of the Revolution. Her book is cited as a source in all major studies of Mayakovsky and his circle yet, until now, has not been published in English.

When I first found the book in the British Library I did not, at the time, realize how rare the 1939 first edition is. Most of that imprint (published by Editions Sociales Internationales) was confiscated and destroyed by the Gestapo during the Nazi occupation of Paris: hardly surprising given that Triolet - herself both Russian and a Jew - was by then married to the writer Louis Aragon. Both were key figures in the Resistance and the Communist movement.

The work was re-published by Pierre Seghers in 1945 - the same year that Triolet won the Prix Goncourt for her work as a novelist. Nevertheless I have used the 1939 edition to make this translation, mindful of the little book's own peculiar place in twentieth century history as I opened its faded yellow cardboard covers.

Though Triolet wrote exclusively in French from 1937 onwards, she was born into the comfortable, petit-bourgeois, Russian-Jewish Kagan family in Moscow in 1896. She left Russia to marry a French soldier, André Triolet, in late 1917... restless, curious and unable, by her own admission, to cope with the privations and epidemics which characterized the period immediately following the Revolution. The marriage, unsurprisingly, failed... though she chose to keep her first husband's name.

Triolet's second marriage - to the poet Louis Aragon - endured until her death in 1970. It was partly due to his "Elsa" poems, as well as the success of her own works, that she became something of a literary superstar in post-war France. Both writers were leading members of the PCF (Parti Communiste Français) until their unwavering support for Stalin, despite his increasingly draconian methods, alienated them from their comrades at home.

Triolet's life was one of adventure, courage, determination and conviction. She seems to have been a very private person, despite her high profile in later years, capable of ruthlessness and often described as "cold". Nevertheless, she counted many of the best-known artists, writers and thinkers of her age among her friends including, of course, Vladimir Mayakovsky.

Vladimir Vladimirovitch Mayakovsky (1893 - 1930) was arguably the most important influence on the young Elsa Triolet. He encouraged her as a writer and introduced her to Aragon. They had had a brief romantic liaison when she was just 16 years old and remained friends. The connection was permanently consolidated in 1915 when the poet met, and instantly fell in love with, Triolet's elder sister, Lili Brik.

From their first meeting on what Mayakovsky famously described as "a most joyous date" his life was inextricably linked with those of Lili and her husband, Osip Brik. Inspired by the idea of a "new family" model, as outlined in Chernechevsky's book *What is to be Done?*, the three lived together for 15 years until Mayakovsky's death by his own hand in 1930.

Writing to Lili Brik in 1939 Triolet affirmed that her newly published memoir presented an "utterly convincing picture of Mayakovsky," and added, "For the first time in my life I have the sense of having done something truly worthwhile."

Triolet's reasons for writing this book seem to have been both personal and political. On a personal level she retraced her own past whilst revealing to her French readers and peers an intellectual pedigree of which she was evidently proud. On a political level, Mayakovsky's status needed to be firmly established and maintained, both in the Soviet Union and abroad: in the years following his death there had been a rapid and efficient movement to obliterate his name and work from the Soviet cultural arena. It was not until 1935 that Lili Brik was able to convince Stalin that her lover had been the true Poet of the Revolution. The leader's statement to that effect, reported in Pravda, ensured the official re-establishment of Mayakovsky as a popular and literary icon.

Lili's own status, as the poet's "widow", had also been disputed. Until Stalin's definitive statements of 1935, an actress, Veronika Polonskaya, had been openly paraded in the role. Whilst it is true that she is mentioned in the poet's suicide note and had a brief affair with him immediately prior to his death, there could be no comparison between her relationship with him and Lili's own - hence Elsa's insistence in her memoir that Lili was "*the* woman" in the poet's life.

Triolet's omissions, however, are as telling as what she includes. She does not, for example, address the poet's increasing disillusionment with the path the Revolution was taking: in 1929, a few months prior to Mayakovsky's suicide, Trotsky was exiled and Stalinism consolidated. Triolet and Aragon maintained an unwavering devotion to Stalin right up until his death in 1953 and could not countenance any criticism of him. Nor does Triolet mention the refusal, in September 1929, of Mayakovsky's application for an exit visa. She must have known about this for he was on his way to Paris where he intended to marry his last "big love" - a White Russian emigrée called Tatiana Yakovleva. The political fallout of such a liaison was unthinkable, both for the authorities and the Briks.

This book was only the second work Triolet had written in French: the language is informal and simple but none the worse for that; the content is sometimes uneven. These factors lend the work its emotional immediacy and are an intrinsic part of what makes it lively and sincere. I have tried to reproduce Triolet's style, as well as the actual content of her book, as accurately as possible.

The extracts from Mayakovsky's verse are new translations from the Russian (see acknowledgements).

The transliterations and versions of names I have used are Triolet's and may differ from those found in other works on the subject.

Susan de Muth, London, 2002

Preface

Mayakovsky was born on the 7th July 1893 in the Georgian village of Bagdadi. His father was a forester. He was the son of tall trees and the beauty of the Caucasus. He grew to be taller, stronger, more remote than other men. He died in 1930, felled at his height.

Few men have left such a deep impression on those who survived them. The sight of his imposing figure roaming the streets is missed just as much in Moscow today as it was the day after he died. His audience, mostly young people, still lament the fading of his resonant voice. The front pages of newspapers are bereft of his verses. Wherever there are people who need to be shown how to love, how to protest, defend and fight, Mayakovsky is missed. Missed wherever genius is required. He is as unforgettable as an amputated limb: you become accustomed to not having him around but you always remember what it was like when you did...

You still think you see him on the streets of Moscow. A whole head taller than everyone else. Such a magnificent head: a large, round skull; long, hollow cheeks and that strong jaw... brown eyes under expressive eyebrows that were never still, beneath a forehead furrowed with one, short, deep, vertical line. Eyes like a good, faithful dog, touching, and so gentle... yet those very same eyes could be horribly indifferent, even cold. So he strode about, those solid legs bearing a strong torso with impressive shoulders. He would walk down Tverskaya Street towards the big square which they've named after him. When you hear the bus conductor say "Mayakovsky Square" or when "Mayakovsky Station" is announced in the luxurious new Moscow Metro you realise that the name hasn't lost any of its impact. It is still the name of a man whose voice is heard inside by thousands of people. His warm hand, his words, his expressive face are forever preserved in the memory of this city.

Mayakovsky's work has already become part of the classics, yet it's still up to date. It's classic because his indisputable genius is now recognised by the whole nation. It's bang up to date because everyday life and the kind of problems encountered in Soviet Russia today throw up reasons to quote him all the time. Love, Revolution, War and Peace, the tiny details of everyday life... there were no minor or major issues in Mayakovsky's poetry. The slogans he wrote for the Cultural Education Department, the publicity poems he wrote for nationalized industries, are deeply etched in people's minds... and they still find them funny. Nor has his love poetry lost its devastating power and his satirical poems still make people feel that somebody's there for them, fighting their corner, ready to flatten the things they hate. Many of his poems will offer excitement, inspiration and hope to future generations.

He had an apartment in a little two-storied house which has now been turned into the Mayakovsky Museum. The rooms were so tiny that every time he moved you thought he'd send the walls flying apart. At the bottom of this little house, on the adjoining brick wall someone has painted, in huge letters:

ALL MY THUNDERING POETIC MIGHT
        I GIVE TO YOU
                THE ATTACKING CLASS

The profession of his faith.

one

Mayakovsky's father was dead*. The family moved to Moscow. Gloomy, destitute. 1906 - 7, Mayakovsky was still at school. At thirteen, fourteen, he developed a passion for philosophy, especially Hegel. And Natural History. But above all for Marxism. In 1908, at fifteen, he joined the Bolshevik Party (then known as the Russian Socialist Party). He was arrested for the first time, accused of writing political tracts, then released. A year of militant activity. Arrested a second time for helping some women attempt an escape from Novinski Prison in Moscow. He got a sentence. During his 11 months in prison (he was fifteen, sixteen) he developed a voracious appetite for literature. He read modern works and the classics: Byron, Shakespeare, Tolstoy. Released from prison in 1910 he was faced with a dilemma:

> **What's the best way for me to confront the old order? When the Revolution comes wouldn't it be better if I had some formal qualifications?**
> **I went to see party comrade Medvedev and told him: 'I want to create a Socialist art form.' Serioja couldn't stop laughing: 'You haven't got the guts !'**
> **I still reckon he underestimated my guts.**
> **I stopped my militant activities and began studying.**
>
> *I, Myself (1928)*

He didn't think himself capable of writing poetry, so he decided to concentrate on painting. He got into the Beaux Arts in 1911. He was thrown out in 1914 having taken no notice of warnings to give up his subversive ways from the principal, Prince Lvov.

---
*see notes at the back of this book

I was at school. Mayakovsky was still at the Beaux Arts, starving, and part of a group which would later be known as the "Futurists". They were going round proclaiming that Mayakovsky was a poet of considerable genius before he'd even written a word. "Now," David Burliouk told him - Burliouk was the oldest among them, a portly person who wore a monocle, a frock coat and had a fringe like a horse's - "now go and get on with it so you've got something to show." Mayakovsky started writing then and there.

I met him at a friend's house. To me he seemed gigantic, incomprehensible and insolent. I was only fifteen and quite scared. Some time later he turned up at my parents' house. He'd sold his first poem - *The Objects Revolt** (which I've never managed to track down since, unless he changed the name). The point is, he'd spent the money on getting "kitted out". He'd got his mother (poor woman) to run him up a lemon yellow blouse* which came half way down his hips and which he wore unbelted with a big, black cravat. A tall hat, an elegant overcoat, and a cane completed the outfit. He had his photograph taken dressed like this. I still have a postcard of it with "The Futurist, Vladimir Mayakovsky" written on it.

He presented himself thus attired at the house of my rather nice but very bourgeois parents. I remember little about this first visit except that the maid was extremely alarmed. Not yet sixteen, I had enough composure to make out to my parents that it never even occurred to me that Mayakovsky would be anything other than welcome in our home.

He came round nearly every day, disarmingly polite to my mother, saying only what was strictly necessary to my father, so that everyone almost overlooked the yellow blouse.

My parents resigned themselves wearily and Mayakovsky was more or less accepted into the household. He used to do his drawings* at our house - his bread and butter at the time - and stay for dinner.

If I wasn't in, he'd leave his visiting card - the size of a book cover and completely taken up with his name in huge yellow letters. My mother would often return these cards to him saying, "Vladimir Mayakovsky you've forgotten your signboard", rather like that song Charles Trenet sings nowadays: "Excuse me, Sir, you've forgotten your horse".

Mayakovsky was courting me. He didn't talk a lot but was constantly muttering, suddenly blurting out lines and utterances, maybe checking his compositions... I wasn't particularly interested in this interior labour going on beside me and hardly even realized that he was a poet. He'd often ask me to play the piano and would then pace about behind me for ages, making gestures... ours was a very musical household, the walls, windows, furniture were saturated, soaked, heavy with sound. My mother, an excellent pianist, often brought together quartets, trios, or two pianos played together by four or eight hands. At such times my father would put on his coat and hat. Those two grand pianos were like pure-blooded, noble beasts among the frippery of our petit-bourgeois apartment. Instead of family portraits we had life-size representations of Tchaikovsky and Wagner looking down at us from the walls, and some bronze bas-reliefs of Mendelssohn and Meyerbeer... my mother made a pilgrimage to Beyreuth every year like a faithful Moslem off to Mecca.

All through my childhood I went to sleep to the sound of music: my mother used to wait until everyone had gone to bed and then play the piano with the soft pedal on. She composed music too. That was my radio at the time. Music was as necessary to me as running water - something you notice only when it's not available any more.

Mayakovsky liked music as a background for working but didn't care to actually listen to it. He hated concerts. Once he and Burliouk went to a Rachmaninov concert as he recorded in *I, Myself*:

> **Posh concert. Rachmaninov's *Island of the Dead*. Insufferable melodic tedium. I fled and so did Burliouk a minute later. We laughed like mad and went for a stroll. Conversation. From Rachmaninov boredom to school boredom, from school boredom to the entire range of classical boredom. David had the anger of a master who has out-paced his peers. I the fervour of a Socialist anticipating the inevitable demise of the old. Thus Russian Futurism came into being.**

So it turned out that Rachmaninov, Boecklin and the *Island of the Dead* all played a part in the birth of Russian Futurism and became symbols of the petit-bourgeoisie for Mayakovsky who used them as such in his poems 13 years later!

But he was really impressed with certain songs, like one which went "Hard hearted Hannah/the vamp of Savannah..." songs with the rhythm of alcohol and Spring.

It was getting late and my mother came down in her dressing gown, closed the piano lid firmly and told Mayakovsky it was time for him to go home to bed. My father had been asleep for ages. She had to return several times before Mayakovsky slowly started putting on his coat in the lobby. He was scared of the caretaker who'd have to get up to open the gates for him. Climb out of his lovely warm bed in the middle of winter, open the door with the cold outside, face glacial blasts of frozen air, his hand stuck on the frosty metal handle... all these factors made a tip absolutely obligatory. Mayakovsky didn't have the necessary ten or twenty kopecks. I wanted to give them to him and could see the battle raging within: should he face the wrath of the caretaker or take money from a woman? He picked up the little silver coin and then dropped it back on the table in front of the mirror, picked it up, put it back... and finally left it. Now that required courage!

The next day he came round again and said to my mother, "Yesterday I just waited long enough to be sure you were asleep then climbed up a rope ladder and came back in through the window." My mother looked at him with a weak smile, wondering if he hadn't simply used the stairs.

My sister, Lili, arrived while all this was going on. She was married and living in Petrograd. One day she asked me what was going on with Mayakovsky. Why did he come round all the time and was I keen on him? She said the whole thing was upsetting our mother and making her cry. What? Making mother cry? Why hadn't anyone told me? And when he phoned me next I simply told him that I couldn't see him any more... because it made my mother cry.

It was several months before we attempted to meet again. I was spending the summer in the country and used to turn up at our rendezvous two or three hours late in the vague hope that he'd get tired of waiting for me. As a further precaution I took along an aunt. But he'd be there, at his post near the little station, standing with his legs crossed, a cigarette glued to his big lower lip, his head held high... and his eyes dull with rage.

I then got the bright idea of seeing him without my mother's knowledge. We'd have to meet somewhere less public than the station, preferably in the evening. Or I could simply go off to Moscow for the day and see whoever I liked without anyone finding out.

In Moscow the empty apartment smelt of mothballs. Footsteps, voices, echoed eerily now that the carpets and curtains had been removed. It was a haunted house with big white dust-sheets over the furniture and the two grand pianos... the hanging lights veiled with gauze which wafted beneath the ceiling, the windows open to the sky... and the large form of Mayakovsky roaming about.

It was during one of our summer evenings in the countryside near Moscow that I first really "heard" the verses Mayakovsky was reciting to himself. We were walking along side by side in the dark, down a wide lane between the fences of two rows of villas. Mayakovsky, absorbed and distant, suddenly burst out with some verses in a loud voice. I won't quote them because no translation could ever convey their overwhelming pathos. Mayakovsky's poems are completely impossible to translate and my attempts to do so elsewhere in this book are only to appease my conscience and with little hope of success.

I stopped, turned to stone. I suddenly realised not only that Mayakovsky wrote poetry but that it was absolutely brilliant! "Ah ha!" said Mayakovsky, triumphant but scornful, "so you *do* like it!" And late into the night, in front of some villa's wooden fence, he recited his poems to me... I was wild with mixed emotions... to think that I'd had all this beside me for such a long time and hadn't even known it. But now I wanted more and more... he was in the process of writing *Cloud in Trousers* and it was verses from that poem which convinced me Mayakovsky was a poet but I also recall, I don't know why, this poem* that started with the lines:

Listen!
Since they light up the stars at all
someone must think they're necessary?
Someone wants them to be there?
Someone says these bits of spit
are pearls?

Maybe it's because the real night was black and star-filled.

I loved poetry. At an age when most kids take a dolly to bed I was already dragging two great volumes there: Lermontov and Pushkin. These had a lot to offer - you could read them and also colour in the illustrations. And as children like stories best that they already know by heart I never left off reading and re-reading the pages of these two books. Later I passed lightly and disdainfully over the so-called "decadent" poets and arrived, unimpressed, at the Symbolists: Brioussov, Balmont, Blok. They had a sort of patina over which you could glide agreeably... but nothing ever caught. For my generation the Symbolists were already a known quantity and we wouldn't have dreamt of fighting for them. They were recognized poets, part of the establishment. We needed an Earthquake and this Earthquake was Mayakovsky. Those of us who felt the grip of his poetry had all the passion, endurance and conquering zeal of true pioneers.

I talked about Mayakovsky's poetry whenever I got the chance. I discussed it, I defended it, I nearly lost my voice! It was like an election campaign and I had all the zeal and elation of someone not yet seventeen who truly believes that poetry is the meaning of life. It was absolutely clear to me that he was a Genius. I had never been able to remember a single line of verse before but now I could recite whole pages of Mayakovsky. They engraved themselves in my memory.

"Incomprehensible" is how the intellectuals and 'aesthetes' described his work with genuine hatred: yet they understood enough to infer that it was somehow directed at them, a protest, like the yellow blouse... designed to flabbergast the bourgeoisie. Then they said things like "Mayakovsky's just a lout, he's so unrefined, an absolute megalomaniac - have you seen what he's called one of his poems? *Napoleon and I*! He thinks it's clever to be so cynical as to tell everyone that he cheats at cards and is nothing more than a low-class pimp."

You,
who have only one worrying thought:
'Do I look good when I dance?'
look at the fun I'm having,
me,
a low-life pimp
and card sharp.

You -
all gooey with the schmaltz
you've been blubbering over
for centuries -
on you I turn my back,

**sticking the sun
into my wide-open eye
for a monocle**

                                                Cloud in Trousers (1915)

"It's perfectly OK to be a non-believer," they went on, "we're atheists ourselves after all - but there are limits! It's simply not gentlemanly to come out with stuff like 'Jesus Christ is savouring the perfume of my soul's sweet forget-me-nots'!"

**I, who sing praises
to the Machine and to England,
might just be
the thirteenth apostle
in a most ordinary Gospel.**

**And while my voice
goes bawdily booming,
day and night,
from hour to hour,**

**maybe
Jesus Christ
is savouring then the perfume
of my soul's sweet forget-me-nots**

                                                Cloud in Trousers

But the big argument was always about whether or not his poetry was totally incomprehensible. The debate raged for many years and Mayakovsky addressed it several times in articles he wrote, in particular one entitled *The workers and peasants don't understand you* (1928):

I've yet to see someone show off by saying "I'm so intelligent - I don't understand arithmetic, or my own language, or grammar".

But they joyfully shout : "I don't understand the Futurists!" That clarion call has gone up again and again over the past fifteen years, always just as excited and happy.

On the basis of this single statement whole careers have been built, lecture theatres have been filled and people have founded entire movements.

....

Simply stating "we don't understand" is not, actually, a verdict. A verdict would be: "We've worked out that it's nothing but a load of gibberish", and this would have to be accompanied by dozens of lofty examples, recited from memory and in a melodious voice.

No-one comes up with that.

There's all sorts of demagogy and speculation on the theme of Incomprehension.

The main propositions of this demagogy, delivered in the most self-important manner, are diverse.

Here are some of them:

- "Art and Literature that only speak to certain individuals are of no use to us. True or not?"

It's true and not true.

They can be the very seeds and carcasses of Art for the masses.

Example - Khlebnikov's poetry. In the beginning only seven of his Futurist comrades could understand it but for the past decade it has electrified numerous other poets, and now the Academy wants to bury it by publishing it as an example of classical literature.

- "True Proletarian Soviet Art must be readily understandable by the People. Is this true or not?"

It's true and not true.

It's true, but has to be qualified with reference to the times and propaganda. Art is not, of itself, art for the masses. It can only become that as a result of many forces pulling together: critical analysis to establish a work's validity and usefulness; judged useful, mass distribution via the Party machine; that distribution itself being correctly timed. Then there's the extent to which the matters addressed in the book accord with the way ideology is developing among the masses .

The higher the quality of the book, the more it will be in advance of history.

....

The comprehension of the masses is achieved as a result of our struggle, not the blouse in which the random writings of some literary genius or another are hatched.

You have to learn how to organise a book's being understood.

- "The classics - Pushkin, Tolstoy, are readily understood by the masses. Is it true or not?"

It's true and not true.

Pushkin was actually only entirely understood by his own class, by that part of society whose language he employed, whose ideas and feelings also inspired him.

We can never really know if the masses of his day, the peasants, understood Pushkin for the simple reason that they couldn't read.

....

> I have read for peasants, in the palace of Livadia. Last month I read in the docks at Bakou, at the Schmidt factory at Bakou, at the Chaoumian Club, at the working men's club at Tiflis, I've read to metal-workers in their lunch-hour standing on a piece of equipment to the accompaniment of hissing machinery.
>
> I quote from one of many reports made by factory committees:
> "At the end of his reading, Comrade Mayakovsky addressed the workers and asked them for their opinions of his work and how much of it they had understood. A motion was proposed that the work was totally comprehensible. The vote in favour was unanimous except for one - and when the worker in question was asked about this he declared that he understood the work better now that the author had read it than when he read it himself at home. 800 people were present."
> The person who wrote this report was the one who counted the votes.

I quote from this article, written in 1928, to show just how tenacious this myth about incomprehensibility really was, as well as how Mayakovsky strove to prove that it didn't originate from the workers or the peasants but from the bourgeoisie and a particular type of intellectual who always viewed him as a vicious enemy and continued to do so until his death.

Nowadays we can all understand these poems easily - the language is as familiar as our mother-tongue - but at the time I'm talking about that was definitely not the case. The first poems he wrote - in 1912 - are his most obscure. The way he cut words short, his concise style, the innovative structure of his sentences, the creation of totally new words, it was too much to take on board all at once... especially when people couldn't be bothered to make the effort in the first place.

His poems also looked strange when they were printed: he made up for the inadequacy of punctuation by cutting up his lines. This also enabled him to indicate the stresses and intonations which were so much part of his oratory style.

Mayakovsky had discovered the key to his work - his voice! The verses were made to be bellowed out. At hundreds of readings all over Soviet Russia he showed how his poetry should be declaimed. Everyone who heard him started imitating his delivery, reciting his poems to others, and they in turn did the same. That's how his work, and the way to interpret it, was distributed orally... and still is today. Mayakovsky's poetry spread like wild fire throughout the USSR.

His voice! That was another thing all those types who thought poetry should be read by lamplight had against him. Not that anyone dismissed their point of view, not even Mayakovsky who answered it thus:

> **The revolution does not mean the end of tradition. The revolution is not about destroying things but rather improving on what it has conquered using technology and pragmatism.**
> **The book will never be a substitute for recital. The book in its time replaced the manuscript but the manuscript was just the way books began. The rostrum, the platform, will always have a role but a much wider audience can now be reached via the radio. The radio, there's the way forward (one of them anyway) for the word, for the watchword, for poetry. Poetry is no longer for the eye alone. The**

revolution has given us the word you can hear, poetry you can hear. Only a lucky few ever got to hear Pushkin speak - and how inspiring that must have been -well, everyone would have that opportunity now.

Lecture, 1927

Essentially, Mayakovsky liked to be understood by as many listeners as possible. Even in the era of Futurism, when the problem of whether or not a wider audience could understand his poetry was simply not an issue, Mayakovsky never used "Zaoum"* - 'transmental language' - employed very brilliantly by Khlebnikov for example. There are still some poets using it today - whose talents are more debatable. Sometime round 1923 Gorky attended a "Zaoum" reading and said that he felt so embarrassed at having been present that if he later met someone else who'd been there he found himself behaving as if they'd both been in a brothel at the same time... horribly self-conscious, a bit ashamed, tittering ridiculously and dealing playful little stomach-punches.

In the last speech he ever gave Mayakovsky said that he thought the poems he wrote in 1912 were his most obscure and that it was these which most often caused the question of incomprehensibility to be raised:

Once it had been suggested to me that my poems weren't readily comprehensible   I committed myself to writing in such a way as to be understood by the largest possible number of listeners.

Shorthand record of speech, 25th March 1930

As early as 1920 Mayakovsky was already saying that he no

longer considered himself a Futurist. In 1923 however, he announced that he would stick with the term because Futurism had become a kind of flag for so many people. Later he drew attention to the fact that Futurism and the *Lef** had become inextricably linked in the minds of the public. The *Lef*, represented by a magazine of the same name, edited by Mayakovsky and his friends, underwent some changes itself and folded in 1927.

In 1928, during a speech about Party policy on Literature, we see Mayakovsky move closer to VAPP* despite that organisation's openly stated opinion of him - that he was nothing but a 'fellow traveller' compared with the real proletarian poets:

> **I consider myself a proletarian poet and that the proletarian poets from VAPP are in fact *my* fellow travellers. I'm not saying this because I want to lead the Lef camp into confrontation with other factions who are trying to gain the upper hand politically... I readily admit that the faded glad rags of the Lef are going to have to be changed.**

In February 1930, at a conference organised by the Proletarian Writers of Moscow, he attacked the "Constructivists":

> **They've completely overlooked the fact that apart from the Revolution itself there's the whole class leading it to take into consideration. They're just recycling the same old images and making the same mistakes as the Futurists - more concerned with style than content. It's just an attempt to curl the few remaining hairs on the bald old pate of outmoded verse and this isn't at all acceptable in proletarian poetry.**

At exactly the same time - February 1930 - that's to say two months before his death, he officially joined the RAPP* which later degenerated into a sort of disgusting sect.

Clinging to things which were once innovative but which have now gone badly out of date - that's what I call getting old. Like Surrealism - a development already overtaken by Romanticism - which still hangs on like an elderly coquette incapable of aging gracefully. Mayakovsky wasn't like that and I am reminded of his lines in *About This* (1923):

I'll get old four times
    four times grow young again
        before I give the grave its due.

His extraordinary, vital flexibility meant he never got stuck in one 'movement' and when such a 'movement' became stagnant he knew it and moved on.

I want to return to the period 1912 - 1913 and those first controversial poetry evenings with Mayakovsky, Burliouk, Khlebnikov and Krioutchionikh. I didn't know any of them personally then but they came across as a pretty riotous bunch* despite the fact that their audience was mostly composed of aesthetes and Symbolists. They had produced a manifesto which they'd all signed called *A Slap in the Face of Public Taste*. Mayakovsky used to give readings, wearing his yellow blouse, and I remember these being something like boxing matches with people shouting, heckling and whistling... but he'd keep his head, showing off, thundering, yelling at the crowd.

There was an evening to elect a "King of the Poets" - I think it was 1914. A series of poets took part, I can't remember exactly which ones. I think Balmont was there among others, and certainly Igor Severiannine* since it was he who won.

Mayakovsky was in a total frenzy, he'd nearly lost his voice from his slanging match with the public. He was absolutely incredulous when he wasn't made "King". Who ever gives Severiannine a thought today? But he was the star of the show that night and the whole hall applauded him wildly. He was characteristically cool and undemonstrative, pale-faced in a black frock coat, holding a red rose out in front of him like a candle.

> **Out of the cigar smoke**
> **the drunken face of Severiannine**
>   **stretched**
> **like an elongated liquor glass.**
>
> **How dare you call yourself a poet**
> **little mediocre thing**
> **twittering like a quail?**
>
> **This world deserves**
> **a set of knuckle-dusters now -**
> **smashing in its skull.**

Cloud in Trousers

This all happened in the hall at the Polytechnic Museum where Mayakovsky would later take his audiences by storm at the height of his glory. I think this was the one and only time Mayakovsky lost his sang-froid in front of a crowd. There was a period when he was getting regularly booed by his audiences but he was undaunted by this apparent lack of success - in fact he seemed delighted and viewed such a lively set-to as a kind of victory. He loved manipulating the audience and it was no holds barred once he started baiting the dragon before him...

I've only ever seen one man - Mayakovsky - who could totally "possess" a room. He played with the audience, teased it, taunted it like a mad bull and could always make it go in the direction he wanted. God help any spectators who were stupid enough to confront him - they soon found themselves flattened on the tiles, knocked out by his arrogance, his casual manner and haughty humour. To the end of his days he gave hundreds of readings and lectures all over the USSR and in every audience there would always be a little group who would gang up against him in some sort of spiteful alliance... and who would end up themselves as the general laughing-stock.

At the end of his readings members of the public would write questions on scraps of paper and throw them onto the stage. In his autobiography *I Myself* (1928) he wrote:

> **I've collected nearly 20,000 questions from audiences. I'm thinking of a book: *The Universal Answer*. I know what's going on in the minds of the reading public .**

But he was impervious to antagonism from the audience. What actually made him nervous was the process of reciting itself, whether or not there was a mass of pink blobs in front of him... a mass who would find themselves absolutely overwhelmed by the moving lyricism of his orator's verse, his preacher's poems, reverberating with the strength and volume of a cathedral organ.

In 1913-1914 the press was interested only in wounding Mayakovsky. In 1914 he began to contribute regularly to the humorous journal *Satirycon*. In the same year he read extracts from *A Cloud in Trousers* to Gorky. Gorky was very moved and started weeping, overjoyed at this discovery of a new genius. When he brought out his review *Letopis* (The Chronicle) in 1915 he took Mayakovsky on as a regular contributor.

two

1915/16/17. I had lost my father. I was living alone with my mother in another house, in another part of Moscow. I had new friends, new passions. After school I went to Architectural College and my head was full of Mathematics and Painting. In the meantime Mayakovsky had become "Uncle Volodya" where I was concerned and what I felt for him was unlimited friendship*... when I thought about him at all.

He was living in Petrograd. I saw him whenever he came to Moscow for a few days or when I went to visit my sister Lili in Petrograd. It was through coming to visit *me* at her place that Mayakovsky got to know Lili*.

I went to Lili's nearly every holiday. In 1915 there was a Christmas Eve party and she had a Futurist Christmas tree. They'd covered the walls of their apartment with bed sheets for the occasion and the tree was hanging upside down from the ceiling. When the candles on it were lit it looked like a beautiful green candelabrum, twinkling with angel hair and glass trinkets. The two small rooms were lit with candles, there were candles everywhere, the ones on the dining room table were stuck in circles on some wooden shields they'd bought in a toy shop. The whole idea was that nothing would be everyday. The guests wore costumes and lots of make-up so that they wouldn't look how they usually did. Bourliouk seemed comparatively normal for once in his frock coat and lorgnette. Khlebnikov was there, stooping and shy, looking like a "big, sick bird" as Shklovsky put it. Shklovsky was there himself, he had his hair like a sailor's then - in black curls. The Futurist poet Vassili Kamenski, Mayakovsky's companion since the very first Futurist battles, was there - an extremely blond boy with the blue eyes of a sea-captain and the flabby mouth of a liar. He had his eyebrows a magnificent blue and drawings on his face to match - a little bird adorned his cheek. He wore a spoon in his button-hole. He was my neighbour at dinner.

The dining room was so tiny that once all thirty of us were seated we had our backs rammed up against the wall and our chests against the table; the dishes could only be brought as far as the door and we handed them down from there as best we could. At the end of the evening my neighbour, Vassili Kamenski, asked me to marry him. Actually, proposing was second nature to him and in his time he got married as many times as he was legally allowed. I immediately told absolutely everyone about it and from then on he was always known as "the fiancé". Mayakovsky really liked him as a poet and comrade in battle but wasn't at all happy about the idea of me marrying him. Not that I ever even vaguely considered doing so.

Back in Moscow I soon met up with Kamenski again. He told my mother all about the fantastic property he owned in the Urals: his house, the forests, the bears, his library. By 2am my mother and I were completely exhausted by his remarkable improvisations. Mayakovsky was back in Moscow too and frowned on Vassia's manoeuvres. "Believe me," he told my mother at every opportunity, "all he owns in the Urals is one flower, one tiny little flower" and he lifted a single finger to illustrate his point. Not that Vassia expected anybody to believe him anyway. It was pure poetry. He had a great talent for Futurist make-believe... and still has.

Mayakovsky wrote to me and I told him my news by letter too... another link between us was the only friend

Mayakovsky had at the time who wasn't part of the Futurist circle. This was S... a boy who was really different from the rest of them. He came from a well-to-do family and had done a lot of travelling. He was well-dressed and balding even though he was still young. Vaguely Polish, he spoke with a slight accent and was very "westernised": he had that pride, that snobbishness, that emotional restraint and horror of complications that I later found so much of abroad.

Mayakovsky was impressed by him in the same way that he was impressed by well-made, useful foreign goods. His rational turn of mind and his odd sense of humour were respected by the Futurists and though he later became an engineer, he remained close to them, always as ready for a slanging match or a scandal as Mayakovsky himself. He later became the director of a big factory in Leningrad.

S... didn't take Mayakovsky's melodramas seriously at all. That was his role - to take nothing seriously, to be dry and rational. I was troubled by the shadow of suicide that always seemed to stalk Mayakovsky but when I spoke to S... about it he ridiculed both me and my notion. He was probably shocked by the idea of suicide being openly discussed. He used to say, "People who talk about it never do it", but actually many suicides *are* preceded by people saying they're going to do it, as well as by deliberately bungled attempts. This kind of exhibitionism doesn't necessarily end up being just for show. But the whole thing seemed to offend his western sense of "dignity" so he would never face up to it.

In fact Mayakovsky never did talk about it - except in his verse. Suicide, the hereafter, a hereafter that he conceived of as magnificent, grotesque and life-affirming, the necessity of living and above all of making life worth living - these are all themes which interconnect in his poetry. In his poem *To Sergei Esenin* he paraphrased the poet's farewell verses:

There's nothing new in this life about dying
*But then there's nothing newer about living**

writing:

There's nothing hard in this life about dying
But building a life - that's altogether harder

Yet in *The Backbone Flute* (1916) Mayakovsky wrote:

More and more often I think
 might it not be better for me
  to put a bullet full-stop
   to the end of my life?

So today,
 just in case,
  I'm giving a farewell concert.

And in *Man* (1917)

The heart leaps towards the shot
 and the throat yearns for the razor.

My anguish expands into
  incoherent delirium
   about the Demon.
He follows me.
  Beckons me to the water.
   Leads me to the sloping roof.

Snows are all around
           a raid of snows
they whirl up
             stop dead
                        lie still.
And start to fall
            - again! -
                 onto the ice,
                      frozen emeralds.

The soul shivers
                trapped in the ice
and no way out from the ice-floes for it!
Like this, bewitched,
                     I walk by the Neva
one step -
           repeated on the same spot.
Spring forward -
               but again, in vain.

A house has erected itself
                    right in front of my nose.
A pot-bellied dawn has exploded
                    behind the window ice.

There!

A cat meowled
a night light burned
smoking.
I ring the bell -
Apothecary!
Apothecary!
I'm sagging over my sticks of legs.

Thoughts shoot up
              get all entangled,
                            antlers,
tears dirtying the floor.
      I throw myself down lamenting
              my lost paradise.

Apothecary!
Apothecary!
Where can the heart
              moan out
                      this anguish
                            to its end?

Is there any shelter for the jealous
                    in the limitless sky
or in the nightmare of the Sahara
          or in the mad heat of deserts?

Behind the walls
            of these glass bottles
                    are so many secrets.

You have the highest understanding of
                            justice,
Apothecary,
        permit me
           to take my soul
              painlessly
                  into the firmament.

**Hands open.
Skull.
"Poison".
A bone across a bone.**

**Who are you giving this to?
I'm immortal, me,
your singular guest.**

Mayakovsky takes up the theme of suicide again seven years later in his poem *About This* (1923), which has this quotation from *Man* as an epigraph:

**That sparkling thing was once there
And they called it
                        NEVA**

[the following extract is from *About This*]:

THE MAN FROM SEVEN YEARS AGO

**Waves wash the bridge's steel
                            foundations,
it stands immobile,
    terrifying, rammed into
            the sides of the capital
                created by me
                      in despair,
and stands on its towering piers
            a hundred storeys high.**

**It embroiders the sky
               with clamps made of air.**

It has risen from the water
                          in a tumult of steel.

I raise my eyes higher
                          higher
There!
    There!
        On the bridge
            leaning over the railings...

Forgive me, Neva!
            she doesn't...
                      she tells me to go.
Have pity on me!
There's no pity in these galloping waters

It's him!
      Him -
           with back-drop sky inflamed
a man is standing
            tethered by me
he stands
        shaking his bedraggled locks.

My paws over my ears
                      - in vain!
I can hear
        my
            my own voice
voice like a knife
        stabbing holes in my paws.

My own voice -
        pleads
            entreats:

"Vladimir!
        Stop!
                Don't leave me!"

Why didn't you let me
                hurl myself in back then?
I could have
        wrecked my heart on the piers.

I've been standing here for seven years
            staring into these waters
                  tethered to the railings
by the ropes of my lines.
For seven years
those waters
        haven't taken their eyes off me.

Oh when
        when
                is it time for deliverance?

Have you, perhaps,
tried to worm your way into their clan?
Kiss?
      Eat?
           Cultivate a belly?

Are you trying to insinuate yourself
        into their everyday routine*?
                Into their family happiness?

"Don't even think about - "
        His hand jabs, threatening,
            beneath the bridge's dry arches

"- don't even think about escaping!
It was I who summoned you.
I will find you
I will hunt you down
    Finish you off
       Torture you to death."

There,
  in the city,
     fun -
       I hear its thunder.

So what?!
   Tell them to come here,
bring over a decree
   from the Executive Committee.
Confiscate my agony.
      Abolish it.

Until,
  along the Neva's depths,
     Saviour-Love comes to me -
drift on, you too,
     you too will be unloved.
Row on!
   Drown me in household bricks!

HELP!

Stop pillow!
    No use.
Row with paw -
    bad oar.

Bridge getting smaller.
Neva's currents
                carry me
                      carry and carry...
I'm already far away
    I'm maybe a day away
        a day away
             from my shadow on the bridge
but the thunder of his voice
                      is after me,
his threats at full sail
              give chase.
You've decided to forget the Neva's
                    sparkle?
You think you'll replace her?
                    No-one could.
'Til you die
      you'll remember the splish-splosh
            that was splashing in *Man*.

I started screaming:
              Can anyone endure this?!
The storm's bass replies:
              Never in a million years.

Help! Help! Help! Help!
      There on the bridge
            on the Neva
                a man!

About This has Love as its central theme. It rages against the pettiness of everyday bourgeois life like a devastating thunderbolt shooting from the heavens to obliterate a bug. It also reasons for and against suicide:

A trial run would be so easy
just lift your hand
              - in a flash
                    the bullet will blast
a thundering path
            to the life hereafter.

What am I to do
            when I totally
                    with all my heart
believed
        and still believe
                in this life
                    in this world?

FAITH

However
      long
          I have to wait
I can see clearly
            as clear as hallucinations
so much
        that it seems -
            the minute I've got out
                  this rhyme
I'll run up
        the line
            and into a wonderful life.
How about this one?
        or that?
                Is it really up to me?

I can see,
> I can see in detailed clarity,
air on air
> like stone on stone,
impervious
> to crumbling and decay,
>> shining,
towering through the centuries -
the workshop of human resurrections.

There he is
> with his high forehead
>> the silent chemist,
furrowing his brow
> at his experiment.

Book -
> *The Whole World* -
>> looking for a name.

"The Twentieth Century.
Whom shall we choose for resurrection?
- There is a Mayakovsky...
Let's try to find something
> more appealing,
the poet's not handsome enough."

I'll yell
> from this
>> very page
- don't look any further!
> **Resurrect me!**

HOPE

Install a heart in me
        and blood to the outermost veins.
Hammer some thought into my skull.
I didn't live-out my earthly existence
        on this earth
                I never loved-out
                        all that belonged to me.

I was three yards tall
      and what good's a yard to me?
            The little things I did
                  an aphid could have done.

I pushed my creaking pen
              in a tiny room transplanted,
in-squeezed with glasses
        into the spectacle-case of a room.

I'll do whatever you want
                      and for nothing too
clean
        wash
            guard
                run errands
                          sweep
I could even serve you as a doorman -
        do you still have doormen?

I used to be merry -
      but what's the point in being merry
in this concentrate of sorrow?

These days
        if anyone bares their teeth
                it's only to snap.

Should it happen that you feel
            heavy-hearted,
                sorrow-torn
Call me!
    The jokes of a fool may do the trick.
I'll keep you entertained with
            hyperbolic extravaganzas
                allegories too.
Make a buffoon of myself with poems.

I used to love…
      no point digging up what's past.
Painful?
    Let it be…
        You live and treasure the pain.

I also loved beasts
        do you still have menageries?
Let me work in one
            I love beasts -
I can see a doggie
        by the baker's -
                all bald -
I would tear my own liver out -
Come on boy, I'm not stingy, eat this!

…………………………………………………………

LOVE

It may
        may be
                some time
down a pathway
            in the zoological gardens
she too -
        for she loved animals -
              will come to the garden
Smiling
    just like this
the way she is in this photo in my desk.

She's beautiful -
        she'll be resurrected for sure.

Your thirtieth century
        will vanquish flocks
              of heart-rending trifles.

Whatever love is unfulfilled now
  we'll make up for
    with the starriness of endless nights.

In 1927 Mayakovsky wrote *Khorocho!* (Good!). The last part of this poem with its refrain "Good!" is a hymn to optimism and joyfulness. It's as though his life had blossomed little by little in those years from 1916 to 1927.

When I received a note from Mayakovsky* asking me to visit him, "Because my nerves are disintegrating", I didn't waste a second. I left for Petrograd that very evening. I rang S... and told him I was going - he said I was mad and in fact

Mayakovsky was just fed up because he hadn't got anyone to go to the cinema with.

In Petrograd Mayakovsky was renting a room in someone's house. I vaguely recall a rather sinister place, bare and dimly lit. Mayakovsky sat at the table with a glass and bottle in front of him, his long cheeks ashen and even more hollow than usual, his cheekbones jutting out. You could see his skeleton, his jacket was hanging off his bony shoulders. He was spending his days drinking, the door locked.

He received me indifferently. Long silences, monosyllables... I began to ask myself what on earth I was doing there. The tension was unbearable. He paced up and down with a cigarette glued to his lip, chain-smoking, drinking, saying nothing. After a few hours of this I was ready to scream. Why had he asked me to come?

But in the evening, when I wanted to leave, he stopped me. I said someone was waiting for me downstairs and he went berserk. So did I. He worked himself up into a demented fury. I'd sooner have died than not leave. All he could think of doing, as I slammed the door, was to shriek after me, hoarse with rage, "Go to the devil - you and your sister".

A second later he passed me on the stairs, raising his hat as he passed: "Excuse me, Madam".

Mayakovsky knew the painter, Vladimir Koslinski, who was waiting for me in a sledge outside. By the time I got there, Mayakovsky had already forced his way in on our evening. God, how I wanted to get rid of him! The three of us were all squashed up in that sledge which was hardly big enough for two. And the evening was a complete nightmare.

Mayakovsky took everything out on Koslinski. I found myself shooting between extremes, laughing madly one minute and plunging into despair the next.

And he continued to have it in for Koslinski for quite a while after that. On the feast of Saint Vladimir he got so nasty - because I'd been out with another Vladimir on *his* saint's day! - that my sister had to intervene. Lili took my side against Mayakovsky and told him that if he didn't make it up with me and shake hands immediately she would never see him again. And Mayakovsky always gave in to Lili.

Lili's circle, that is the Briks' circle, initially had a strong resistance towards Mayakovsky's poetry - although they didn't realise it. There, as elsewhere, I really had to fight and shout and explain lots of things before they finally condescended to hear him read. But when they did their endorsement of his work was absolute. I remember, for example, the first time he read *War and the Universe* in Lili's apartment in Petrograd. It was 1916. Victor Shklovsky started sobbing, his head on the piano; there was the same kind of collective shiver that's produced by a drum leading troops to the front, a silence hammered by rhythmic steps, a deep sense of despair, the heart in tatters.

three

In his autobiography *I myself* (1928) Mayakovsky wrote:

> **26th February 1917:   Went with the cars to the Duma. Looked in on Rodzianko's office and visited Miloukov.   Didn't have much to say for himself. Also got the impression he stutters. I got fed up with the whole bunch of them after about an hour...**
>
> **October: To stick with it or not? For me (as for the other Moscow Futurists) this question never arose. It is my Revolution. Went to Smolny. Worked. Did everything that came my way.**

What with these events and everything that was going on in my own life, I hardly gave Mayakovsky a thought. Anyway he always relayed everything I told him straight back to Lili. He'd become part of the family.

At the Travel Office, just next to my Architectural College, near the Red Gate and in a building which used to house an exclusive school for young noblewomen, I was given a passport to go abroad. The comrade who dealt with me said: "So, aren't there enough men for you here in Russia? What are you hooking up with a foreigner* for?". Everyone around me was of the same opinion but I didn't listen to a word. Not to anyone. For her own peace of mind my mother decided to accompany me on my journey.

We were to embark in Leningrad. I got there with my heart torn to shreds by leaving Moscow. My ears were ringing with the voice of my old wet nurse. She'd started wailing as though someone had died the minute she saw us getting into the cab with our meagre luggage.

It was July 1918. It was extremely hot. Famine and cholera were decimating Leningrad. There were people dying everywhere you looked. Collapsing in the streets, on tram lines... Mountains of fruit were left to rot because you could get cholera from eating it. Lili and Mayakovsky were staying in the countryside just outside Leningrad. I went to say goodbye to them.

Lili came by herself* to see us off on the boat that would take Mama and me to Stockholm. For many years I was haunted by the vision of Lili as she was at that moment, on the quayside. We were already on the bridge, and she was handing us a packet of meat sandwiches - a big luxury at that time; her red head was thrown back and she was showing us all her strong splendid teeth in a wide, painted mouth. Her round, brown eyes were all lit up and her face had that peculiar intensity of expression which was almost indecently excessive - an intensity she never lost, young or old, when her complexion was miraculous or when it was all wrinkly. People always turned round after her in the street. To reach us she had to stand on tip-toe, her little, child-like feet perilously near a pool of excrement which was probably full of cholera.

The arrival in Stockholm, a city which had not experienced the war. It was wallowing in comfort, drowning in provisions. The sight of all those cakes made me want to vomit and I kept on seeing Lili's little feet, so near that unspeakable puddle.

There had been several cases of cholera on board the boat, the *Angermanland*, which had carried us to Stockholm. We were kept in that city for some time and we had to go to the doctor's every day.

Mayakovsky describes the suffering, struggles, victories and everyday life of these difficult years from 1917 on, in *Khorocho!*. It's a very long poem which goes up to 1927 and culminates in great joy. I have chosen some autobiographical lines which deal with the years 1919 - 1920:

That winter
             thin and grim
                          covered over
those
      who had fallen asleep
                          forever.

How can I put this in words!
And I'll never get anywhere near
       the sorrows of the Volga
                       in these lines...

I take some days
        from a succession of days
                 like a thousand other days
 Days from a grey zone
  flushed out by the years
              themselves neither sated
                              nor starving.

If I've ever written -
            If ever I've said
                          anything worthwhile
it's because I'm in thrall
                    to the eye-skies

of the one I love
round
      and brown
hot
  and charred.

The telephone
         already half crazy
              goes completely insane
and drops this bombshell:
those huge brown eyes
        are being squeezed
              by the swelling of hunger.*

The doctor waffles:
"For the eyes to do their job
    warmth
         and fresh veg are required"

I'm not taking these home
         or making them into soup
I'm taking these two tiny carrots
        to the one I love
holding them by their little green tails.

I've often given flowers
        and sweets
but more than any expensive present
I remember this
        precious carroty gift
            and half a log of birch.

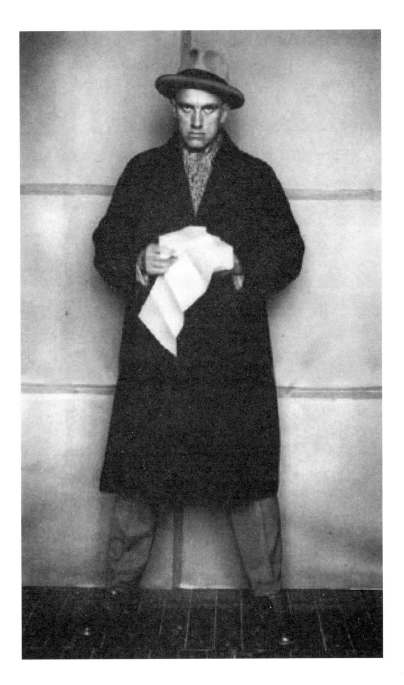

Mayakovsky at one of the many recitals he gave during his extensive reading tour of 1926 and 1927.

Mayakovsky in 1910 when he was attending Stroganovsky Art College, and works by the young Futurist. The portrait of Lili Brik (bottom right) was made in 1915.

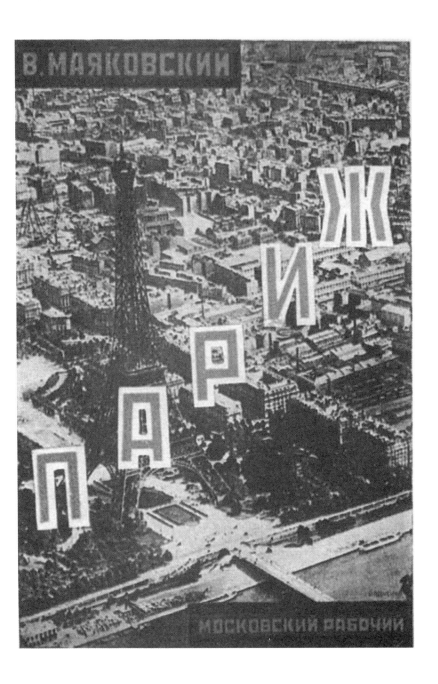

The cover of Mayakovsky's poem cycle *Paris* (1925) written during his visit to Elsa Triolet in November and December 1924.

Elsa (left), Lili (right) and Mayakovsky on the beach in the Crimea, 1916. Note Lili's proprietorial finger on Mayakovsky's hip.

Wet and puny
          under my arm
                  some tiny sticklets
scarcely thicker
          than average browlets.

Her cheeks were swollen,
                  her eyes ... slits.
Greens and caresses
          nursed them back to health.
Bigger than saucers
        those eyes watch the Revolution.

....

The snow falls
          behind a window
the snow's step
          is silent , soft
and the rock of the Capital
                is white and naked
and the skeleton of the forest
                is stuck to the rock.

Now, from behind the forest,
        into the shawl of the sky
                creeps the louse of the sun.

December
        dawn
                exhausted and late
rises over Moscow
                like a typhoid delirium.

The clouds
        have left
                for better-fed countries.
Beyond the clouds
        lies the coast-line of America
reclining
      lapping up coffee
                and cocoa.

In your face -
     fatter than porcine whims
       rounder than restaurant dishes -
from our
      impoverished
             land
                  I hurl this cry:
I love
        this
                country.

You can forget
        where and when
            you grew your belly
and double chin
        but the land
            you have shared
what it is to be hungry with -
that land
        you will always
               remember.

I next saw Mayakovsky in 1922 or '23 in Berlin where we'd arranged to meet up with Lili. I had rented two rooms in a very eccentric place. In one of them there was a stuffed barn owl, a divan embedded in a structure of shelves and a display of various armaments on the wall. In the other there was a huge double bed which also had some kind of weird construction over it.

I kept bumping into Russian friends that time in Berlin... some family, some not related to me but picked up here and there through life and then lost again little by little. As for Mayakovsky, we hardly exchanged a word. Or else he'd be trying to pick a fight with me and Lili would have to intervene, as she did before, to prevent an almighty brawl.

I went back to Paris where I no longer had anyone waiting for me. Mayakovsky visited on several occasions and we tacitly made our peace. I loved going to meet him at the station! He seemed so tall when he got off the train!... You only really notice what someone looks like when you've been apart - even for a little while. And the voice... how strange the voice of an intimate friend sounds when you haven't heard it for some time. He looked monumental as he came towards me along the platform and everyone turned to stare at him: "Come on, let's have a look at you!" he said. "We've been telling everyone in Moscow how pretty you are - I 'd better make sure we weren't lying."

four

I went back to Moscow for a visit in 1925. It was still the Moscow of the NEP*, still suffering, despite the hard years they'd already been through. People who are now in their twenties probably don't remember those days. For them it's completely normal to see Moscow all polished, asphalted, swarming with buses, new cars and nearly-new cars. They already look down on horse-drawn carriages as they do in Paris, they obey traffic regulations and those immaculately dressed militiamen wearing white gloves; they eat cake and buy flowers.

In 1925 Moscow was just beginning to eat cake. They had got that far, they were smiling... but the houses, the little houses of Moscow, whitewashed or coloured like Provençal figurines, some pink, some yellow, were decaying, falling apart, leaning against each other so they wouldn't tumble down, broken windows, gaping roofs. The roads were full of potholes, carriages had ragged upholstery, the very few cars were held together with bits of string, broken-winged, unpolished... the trams jam-packed and looking as if they might topple over at any moment...

Moscow was teeming, overpopulated, bursting at the seams. My sister had overcome the housing crisis by moving out of Moscow to Sokolniki, a large forest which started at the outskirts of the city. She lived in a dacha made of logs - as all the villas outside Moscow were. They had a billiard table. I really don't know how that enormous billiard table ended up there. It was far too big for their normal-sized living room which already contained a piano, a big divan and so on. In summer you could eat on the terrace and there was a garden so the billiard-players could move around without too much trouble but in winter, and on Sundays when a big crowd of friends would turn up, there wasn't any space between the soup tureen and the bent-over player - especially when that player was Mayakovsky. The cat had nowhere to go so it snoozed on the piano. Towards evening a guard-dog called Chanik joined the general mêlée - he was let loose at night and charged in to announce it. He raced around the house with his feet hardly touching the ground and before anyone had worked out what this red flurry could possibly be, had already disappeared. Animals always had a place of honour in Lili and Mayakovsky's home. Just as they did in his verse - whole poems dedicated to them.

They had a series of dogs and Mayakovsky mentioned them all in his work. Latterly the house was afflicted with a French bull-terrier bitch named Bulka. This was a perfectly human creature with all the neuroses of an old girl, who was looked after like a maiden aunt.

I don't want to talk about Mayakovsky's children's books here but they became extremely popular. I will just mention one figure which was recently brought to my attention - that they printed a million copies of one of his poems for children earlier this year [1939].

In summer Sokolniki was pretty lively. People strolled around and sat out in their gardens late into the evening. Winter was a different story. Coming from Moscow at night, the tramway bordered by the big forest heavy with snow, the silence, the whiteness, the deserted streets as wide as the Champs Elysées, a virgin whiteness that no footprint had spoilt, the dachas at the bottom of their gardens, sometimes with a light in the window... the snow-flakes falling from a star-filled sky, snowflakes shaped like stars which always made me think, since childhood, that the stars themselves were falling.

Apart from a few break-ins at the dacha, nothing particularly bad ever happened to us there. This was pretty lucky considering neither the doors nor the windows on the ground floor shut properly. At night we tied bits of string to the door handles and attached these to heavy pieces of furniture, armchairs and so on... the idea being that if anyone tugged at the door they'd pull the furniture over and wake us up... we called these "psychological locks" and in retrospect I think they were quite dangerous because if anyone actually had got into the dacha it would have been better for us if we'd stayed asleep. There were guns all over the place as well - another hazard because people who are suddenly woken up can behave really unpredictably.

Once a friend of ours went out for a walk between the dacha and the tramway and took his revolver with him for protection... When he got back he accidentally let the gun off and the bullet went right through his finger. We had to get him back to Moscow, but in those days it was really difficult to find any kind of transport. It took two or three hours telephoning round before we could get him a lift. We'd all finally gone to bed when we heard someone knocking loudly at the door. Armed with our guns we went downstairs: it was two militiamen who'd come to find out why a gunshot had been heard and to see if we needed any help...

Mayakovsky had a room in town which he used as his study and which doubled as the headquarters of the *Lef*. He worked there, received visitors and sometimes stayed overnight.

He kept it on when the dacha at Sokolniki was abandoned in favour of a miniscule apartment in Moscow which today forms part of the Mayakovsky museum. In 1925 when I went to visit Moscow, Mayakovsky was still abroad and as winter fell I installed myself in his study.

This study was in Loubiansky Passage, near the square of the same name, in the heart of Moscow's poorest quarter. It was on the third floor of a very big, solidly built edifice with smoke-blackened, thick, ugly walls. There were numerous entrances all round the asphalt courtyard. Here in Paris such a building would be called a "cité". The Polytechnic Museum - where the famous election of the "King of the Poets" was held - was nearly opposite.

In one of his 1927 pocket books Mayakovsky wrote:

> **I'm absolutely certain that Loubiansky Passage - where we produce the *New Lef* review and where I live - will end up being called Mayakovsky Passage. You'd never think it now though - the other day I received an invitation from some artistic organisation or other addressed in this lamentable way: 'New Less* Editions, for the attention of Vladimir Vladimirovitch Loubiansky'. Well it's fair enough I suppose, a passage is longer than a writer... especially one who uses short lines.**

At night the main entrance to the cité was closed. The tenants walked past the sleepy yet vigilant eye of the night-watchman. He was majestic, moving slowly, wrapped in a big coat lined with fleece which dragged on the ground behind him and swept the snow. The clock in Loubiansky Square marked the night hours and the snow creaked under the heavy steps of the night-watchman's felt boots. The study was in a flat shared by all sorts of people but was self-contained, above a dark entrance and right next to the stair door. It was very dingy: one single window overlooked the courtyard, the wallpaper was as dark as the big desk at the window, there was a lamp to the left and a narrow sofa covered in slippery black oilcloth. It was nice there, warm and austere, always smelling a bit like an épicerie. The black sofa doubled as a bed and you could feel the coldness of the oilcloth through the sheet which slithered around on it. Mayakovsky must have got his rheumatism on this bed - it never occurred to him to put a blanket under the sheet.

He spent money like water, splashing it about, losing it at cards, yet had no interest whatsoever in comfort or luxury.

He did like things that were really well made though, things that were useful and practical: a good pen, a typewriter, a warm sweater... and he was a connoisseur. When he had the means he went to the best tailor and dressed with the assured good taste of someone who's been used to doing so all his life. But actually all he really needed was his collapsible rubber bath which he took on tour with him, a vast quantity of eau de cologne, and some travelling accessories:

I haven't
        a rouble
                left   from my verse

No cabinet maker
                ever sent furniture
                    over to my house

and apart from
        a freshly-laundered shirt

**to be honest
I need nothing at all**

At the Top of my Voice (1930)

It was in this study in Loubiansky Passage that Mayakovsky died. It is kept exactly as it was on the day of his death.

I didn't witness at first-hand Mayakovsky's rise to stardom. By the time I came back to Moscow in 1925 he was already famous. He was recognised by people in the street and cab-drivers. People would whisper: "Look - it's Mayakovsky... there's Mayakovsky!"

He wrote about this in *New-born Capitals* (1927):

> **A docker in Odessa, having lugged someone's cases on board, said "hello" to me straight away without any sort of introduction and where you might have expected a "how do you do?" came straight out with this: "Tell the boys at Gosizdat* to publish a less pricey version of your Lenin".**
>
> **And once a member of the Red Army, on patrol down Tiflis Road, came over to verify the authenticity of my poetic personage for himself.**

Autographs, adulation, Soviet Youth with him and for him... he contributed to a considerable number of newspapers and magazines. Yet he continued to have problems with the literary 'establishment'. Mayakovsky never gave up and defended his position and his poetry to the end:

> **The aesthetes yell things at me like 'you used to write beautiful poems such as *A Cloud in Trousers***

and now look at your stuff!' Well I've always said that there's poetry which works well on a technical level and then there's the poetry of the masses, armed with quite different weapons - the weapons of the working class. I've never written just any old thing to earn a few bob; but on the other hand I've never refused to write about anything in the news - from the Koulaks* to the rabbit skins currently on sale in the state shops

Shorthand record of speech 25th March 1930

From 1919 - 1922, at the very same time as he was engaged in writing great poems like *150,000,000* and *I Love*, he was also working on what they called the "satirical shop windows" at ROSTA, the Soviet Post Office. In an article published in *New Lef* in 1927, Mayakovsky wrote:

The ROSTA windows are fantastic. A handful of painters are working flat out catering for the needs of a population of 150,000,000: as soon as news comes in by telegraph it's written up on posters; decrees are immediately communicated via the lyrics of popular songs and spread around that way...

It's a new art form, springing directly from everyday necessity: huge posters stuck up in stations, hoardings and empty shop windows. Posters that the Red Army soldiers looked at just before going into battle... not with a prayer but a song.

You can judge the quality of these works for yourselves. The quantity is excessive. I was working until 2am every morning and when I did go to sleep I put a log under my head instead of a pillow so that

I would wake up early enough to draw in Deniken's and Youdenitch's eyelashes in Indian ink. A stupefying majority of the slogans were made up by me too.

In 1923 he wrote *About This*, a love poem and one of his most remarkable works for the perfection of its form, its overall mastery. And at the same time he was making advertising posters for state industries, ordered by unions and officials.

In 1925 he published his great poem *Vladimir Ilyitch Lenin** to commemorate the first anniversary of Lenin's death. This poem, dedicated to the Russian Communist Party, is a fine example of the synthesis of social and human lyricism which was Mayakovsky's own invention.

At every stage of his life Mayakovsky had enemies in literary quarters. There were whole schools and movements opposed to the Futurists and the *Lef*. There were those who thought everyone should write like Pushkin or Tolstoy and there were those who would recognise only the work of proletarian writers. There were some who reproached Mayakovsky for writing propaganda poetry and socio-political poems, who also claimed that he didn't mean a single word of them. Then there were those who criticised him for writing lyrical poems - especially his love poems - because, according to them, they were of no obvious benefit to the proletariat. There were those who complained that he was too devoted to the Party... and those who said he was not devoted enough. Some people said he was finished, empty, without even a hint of his former talent left... (how brilliantly he refuted those charges with the last poem he wrote *At the Top of my Voice* and some others, published posthumously, in which he had achieved an almost supernatural perfection). There were all sorts: reactionaries, sectarians and those who were quite simply jealous.

Mayakovsky did little to soothe this antagonism with his arrogance and his contemptuous epigrams in verse and prose that some people still drag up at every opportunity. Those 'literature officials' were simply blinded by their hatred of this man who was so much their superior and who ground them under the heel of his genius. They didn't even realise what Mayakovsky meant to the nation, to youth... right up to the day of his funeral which became a huge, chaotic pilgrimage. The organizers had never imagined that hundreds of thousands of people would turn up in the streets to march beside his coffin. What did they know, obsessed by their own petty concerns, of the love a whole nation can have for a poet? They hadn't a clue...

Mayakovsky saw through them all. At his last recital before his death he read *At the Top of My Voice* for the first time. The last lines of this poem are:

> **Called to account
>   before the CCC***
>   **of our beautiful future,
> over the heads
>   of ruthless careerists
>   and gangs of opportunistic 'poets'
> I'll be waving
>   all hundred volumes
>   of my party books
>   my Bolshevik party card.**

They persecuted him right up to his death. They printed inadequate editions of his work, they removed his books and his portrait from public libraries. I ran into one of these little 'literature officials' at the 1934 Writers' Congress in Moscow and rebuked him for having blatantly erased Mayakovsky's name from a magazine article, as if the name were somehow dishonourable. He told me: "There is a Mayakovsky cult and we are struggling to keep it down." Who did he mean by "*we*"?!

Not Lenin, at least. In 1922, whilst speaking at the Metalworkers' Congress, he told his audience:

> **Yesterday I came across a poem* by Mayakovsky in Izvestia - it was about politics and officialdom and I must say it's been a long time since these subjects have given me such pleasure. In his poem he completely ridicules meetings and the Communists because they never stop having them. I don't know what this has to do with poetry but as far as politics are concerned I can guarantee that it's absolutely accurate!**

Nor Stalin* either. He recognised Mayakovsky's genius and expressed the opinion that "Mayakovsky is, and will remain, the best, the greatest poet of our Soviet age." He also added that "indifference to his memory and his work is a crime." And little by little, like dead branches, the criticism, the slander, the personal enmity, fell away and the tree of Mayakovsky's glory was allowed to grow... very straight and very tall.

five

He never worked sitting at a table with a pen in his hand. He worked wherever he was, from morning to night: in the street - where he'd roam around for hours; during conversations; while flirting with women... whatever he was doing he brought his work along too, in his mind. This is the main reason that he could come across as sombre, preoccupied and taciturn; and why communication, conversation with him was so difficult.

At the beginning of his poetic career he 'wrote' - if you can call it that - all his poems completely in his head, in his memory. A poem that he'd change ten, even a hundred times, would undergo all these transformations in his head. He crossed out, altered, rewrote a 1500 line poem all in his mind and had perfect recall of each version. And what he eventually committed to paper would be the final draft after a series of drafts which he'd sometimes worked on for months. Later he started noting down words, sentences and verses in his precious pocket-books - calling them his "poetic reserves".

He had a prodigious memory. He not only knew all his own poetry by heart (and that was several books by the end of his life) but also volumes of other poetry both ancient and modern.

In *How Verses are Made* (1926), Mayakovsky gives precise technical details of his poetic method:

> **...You have every right to expect that poets won't take the secrets of their craft with them to the tomb. I'm going to tell you about my work, not as a pedant but as a practitioner.**

....

One thing's for sure - those old 'how to write poetry' manuals won't teach you a thing. They only tell you about traditional ways of writing which have been endorsed simply because they've been in use for ages. It would be more appropriate to call these books not 'how to write' but 'how they used to write'.

To tell you the truth I know nothing about iambics or trochaics and have no interest in the subject. Not that it's particularly difficult, I simply have no use for such things in my work.

....

When it comes to writing poetry there are just a few rules about how to begin. And again, these rules are merely convention. Like chess. The opening gambits are almost identical. But after that you come up with a new strategy. The most satisfying moves are ones you couldn't reproduce in a subsequent game. Only a totally unexpected move will wrong-foot your opponent.

....

From my point of view the ideal poetic work would be something commissioned by the Comintern* with the victory of the proletariat as its climax, using a new vocabulary, expressive and comprehensible to all, composed on a well-equipped table and delivered to the publisher by plane. I have to insist on the plane because the engagement of poetry with contemporary living is an essential aspect of our Industry.

....

The preparatory work for a poem is a continuous activity. High quality work can be achieved only if you have a large number of "poetic reserves" at your disposal.

Here Mayakovsky gives examples of his poetic reserves, rhymes and alliterations, themes such as: the rain in New York; an elderly toilet attendant in an enormous restaurant in Berlin, an American song that needs to be adapted and Russified...

>All these reserves are stored in my head, the most complicated in my pocket-book. I never know how I'm going to use them exactly, only that I will use them. Preparing these reserves takes up all my time. I spend between 10 and 18 hours a day on them and I'm always muttering something. It's this level of concentration that's responsible for the notorious absent-mindedness of poets.
>
>My work on these reserves is carried out with such intensity that 90 times out of 100, I remember the exact place where each rhyme, alliteration, image and so on took its final shape during the whole 15 year period I've been writing.

Here he gives several examples of rhymes and the place each one was composed: the convent at Strasnoi, 1912; an oak tree at Kountzevo, 1914; in a carriage by the harbour, 1917 and so on..

>This "pocket-book" is a compulsory resource if you want to write something worthwhile.
>
>Generally these books are only mentioned after the poet has died, they gather dust for several years then they're published posthumously, long after his "finished works". But for the writer, this notebook is all.
>
>..
>
>It's only the existence of my "reserves", meticulously thought through, that allow me the time to get anything finished. My normal output, for work in progress, is just 8 to 10 lines a day.

Whatever the context, a poet sees every meeting, every billboard, every event solely as raw material to be processed into words.

In the past I was so deeply involved in this work that I became terrified of using up words and expressions that I might want to use in a poem later on... so I became sombre, annoying and taciturn. In 1913 I was on a train and told a young woman I'd just met - to prove the purity of my intentions towards her - that I was not a man, but a cloud in trousers. No sooner had I uttered these words than I realised they'd be perfect in a poem but now might get repeated and squandered. Terribly worried, I subjected the unfortunate young person to at least half an hour's interrogation, asking her the most insincere questions, and only relaxing when I was absolutely certain that my words were going in one ear and out the other. Two years later I used *Cloud in Trousers* as the title of a poem.

....

I walk swinging my arms, muttering quietly, almost wordlessly to begin with, measuring my steps so they don't interfere with my mumbling, then I mutter more quickly, keeping time with my steps.

This is how I perfect my rhythm, the basis of all poetry, the bass-line through the work. Little by little you start to extract the words from this rumble. Some words simply leap away and never come back, others hang around, turning up again and again until you are convinced that one of them has finally found its place (this feeling evolves with experience and is what they call talent). Most often the key word is formed first, the word which does most to convey the meaning of the verse or to establish the rhyme scheme. Then the other words turn

up and take their stations in relation to the key word. When the basics are in place you suddenly sense that the rhythm has gone wobbly - some tiny syllable, some minute sound has gone missing. And you have to start again, refashioning all the words until you end up in a state of delirious exasperation. It's a bit like having an ill-fitting crown put on your tooth: the dentist tries to jam it on hundreds and hundreds of times and it just won't fit, then suddenly he pushes at it one more time and snap! it goes on fine. This comparison is particularly pertinent where I'm concerned because once that crown is fitted I find myself spurting tears of pain and relief (literally!).

....

A man who's picked up a pen for the first time in his life and thinks he can come up with a poem after trying hard for a week will not benefit from reading this book.

My book is useful to anyone who realises that poetry is one of the most difficult undertakings yet wants to be a poet no matter what; anyone who wants to master the mysterious techniques of the poetic process and to pass them on to others.

This is a very lofty conception of poetry... not a luxury or some kind of hobby, not a game for the Gods but something of vital importance and one of the hardest crafts to master. Governed by something more than raw inspiration, writing a poem represented an enormous amount of work for Mayakovsky. He never settled for a "more or less" and his mastery was achieved after years of practising his scales, exercising his voice, training and breaking through barriers, which in turn opened the way for generations of verse-smiths to come.

**I used to think
that books were made like this:
A poet arrives
opens his lips
with no effort
and straight away
this simpleton, inspired,
brings forth a song
to order.**

**But in truth
before they start singing
poets tramp about for ages
getting corns
while the silly flounder of imagination
undulates in the ooze of the heart.**

Cloud in Trousers

One reason I have quoted at length from the pamphlet *How Verses Are Made* is to show how difficult it is to translate Mayakovsky's work... in fact I think it's impossible. For a start there are his rhymes - which didn't even exist until he invented them with his own peculiar ingenious versatility. How can these be represented in a translation? You'd have to retrace the whole process by which Mayakovsky arrived at each word in an entirely different language. This would require years and inconceivable genius.

You'd have to reproduce the rhymes whilst keeping the rhythm, his own mysterious rhythm that he discusses in the pamphlet and which has nothing to do with any known poetic method. You'd also have to keep his economy, compactness and use of abbreviated words which are unique to him and the Russian language. All this as well as making up entirely new words (as Mayakovsky did) and original expressions. All this as well as revolutionising poetry.

Here's what Mayakovsky himself wrote in the preface to a collection of his verse translated into Polish (1927):

> **To my Polish Readers:**
> **Translating poetry is a difficult business, especially my poems. This is the reason that European writers know so little about Soviet poetry. This is even more of a shame since the literature of the Revolution started with verse.**
> **One major reason that it's difficult to translate my poems is that I use a lot of everyday, spoken language. Verses can only be wholly understood if you have a feeling for the whole underlying system of a language because some things, like word-play and puns, are almost untranslatable.**

His method of working irritated some people. There's a certain moral expectation in some quarters - I'm not really sure why - that if you intend to do some work you should get up early, set yourself up in the same place every day and allow yourself no distractions whatsoever. When Mayakovsky was in Paris some people - 'artists' too whom you'd expect to be aware of the fact that there are many ways of working - used to say to me, "Just look at the way this Soviet poet carries on... he gets up at midday and hangs around in nightclubs and cafés... what is it you say in your country? 'If you don't work you don't eat' isn't it? Well that certainly doesn't seem to apply to him!"

They should take a look at the poem cycles Mayakovsky brought back from his Paris trips, and from Mexico and

America where he undoubtedly continued to "hang around in nightclubs and cafés". These poem cycles are among his most accomplished work along with his prose account *My Discovery of America*.

But other people make your reputation for you and Mayakovsky's had been long established; it took root at the time of the yellow blouse and continued to flourish. Ten, fifteen years later, he still hadn't been forgiven that yellow blouse! People were still angry with him and felt that he'd made a mockery of them. They felt obliged to make out he was some kind of lout, not take him seriously, remain sceptical... I remember once in Paris in 1925 I overheard a young person speaking to Mayakovsky after a talk he'd just given: she said, "In two or three years, when you've calmed down a bit, you'll probably be quite good." She was exactly twenty, and extremely pretty. Mayakovsky looked at her, smiled cheerfully, and suggested they spend the evening together. He was less indulgent with men. He would calmly say to some magnificent gentleman, "Go and get us some ciggies will you?" and generally the gentleman would go...

People... people who nibble at you, who nibble at your life with their conjecture, their judgments, gossip and slander... Few men have had to endure as much slander as Mayakovsky - there was a never-ending stream of lies and falsehoods being told about him. He hardly ever talked about this subject but when he did it was always with a sort of deep surprise. It did hurt him. It hurt him a lot, but he'd just shrug and laugh it off. I never once heard him gossip and he never commented on the lives and affairs of other people. Tittle-tattle and backbiting were things that particularly exasperated him.

He wrote the poem *Farewell* in Paris. It's largely composed of overheard conversations in a café and ends with these lines:

> **Listen, readers**
> **When you hear that**
> **Mayakovsky**
> **is thick as thieves**
> **With Churchill**
> **Or that I've just married**
> **Coolidge's maiden aunt**
> **Do me a favour**
> **and don't believe them for once.**
>
> Farewell (1925)

Then there's the speech given just two weeks before his death at the opening of his exhibition *20 Years' Work* which contained these tragic words:

> **I am possessed of a fighting spirit and this leads people to attribute the most amazing dark deeds to me and to accuse me of numerous sins - both real and imagined.**
>
> **Because of this I often have days when I wish I could escape somewhere - anywhere - for a couple of years or even longer just so I wouldn't have to listen to the endless moans and complaints about me.**
>
> **I usually manage to pick myself up, drop the pessimism, roll back my sleeves and start fighting back, insisting on my right to exist as a writer of the revolution, and not to be marginalised.**
>
> **That's the reason for this exhibition - to show that the revolutionary writer is not someone on the fringe whose books are left gathering dust on the shelf... but that the revolutionary writer is a man**

who participates fully in ordinary, everyday life and the construction of socialism.

Shorthand record of of speech 25th March 1930

These are the first lines of the letter he left before dying:

To all of you: I'm going to die. Don't blame anyone and please don't gossip - this stiff really hated that.

Since about half of all conversations consist of gossip, Mayakovsky hated them too - whether they were prattling nonsense or elevated dissertations on the various states of consciousness. He used to say that if people didn't talk so much, human relationships would be much easier and there'd be far less unhappiness about. As for his relations with other people - he preferred to play games with them. He liked cards best, then billiards, then anything - invented games. Preferably for money but also for a variety of incredible forfeits. I once witnessed a fat and extremely respectable gentleman wriggling under the billiard table on his belly because he'd lost a game. One night, in a deserted street in Montmartre, Mayakovsky and some friends started mucking about, throwing Mayakovsky's cane through a big golden crown, a mortuary emblem, sticking up on the outside of a funeral parlour. Rules of the game evolved on the spot and bets were laid. Mayakovsky won the lot - he had a very good eye and apart from that his arm was nearly on a level with the crown.

Mayakovsky played all games well, especially cards and billiards. Maybe he liked games because he found them relaxing, forcing him to think about something else for a while, something other than the work which obsessed him. He also liked gambling, taking risks - in games and in life.*

Then there were women. First of all *the* woman, *his* woman, the one he dedicated all his books to. His obsession with her dominates his love poems, and the others; it is palpable at every stage of his development as a writer and in his farewell letter: "Lili love me."

Dedicating his poems to Lili was not, for Mayakovsky, simply a matter of writing her name at the end of a finished poem as some kind of nice gesture or out of a sense of duty. Every single word of a poem would be dedicated to her - it really would be written *for* her.

Here is an example, taken from the 1916 poem *Backbone Flute*:

> **I will out-dawn
> the sky
> that for smoke
> has forgotten what blue is
> and the storm clouds too,
> tattered like refugees,
> with my last love
> bright as a consumptive's flush.**
>
> **I will drown out
> the roaring
> of the mob,
> who've forgotten what
> home and comfort are,
> with my joy.
> People,
> Listen!**

Get out of the trenches
you can finish your war later.

If
the fight reels on
blood-drunk like Bacchus,
even then
words of love
will not perish.
Dear Germans!
I know
you have Goethe's Gretchen
on your lips.
The Frenchman dies
on the bayonet, smiling
and the shot-down pilot
smiles as he crashes -
for they remember, Traviata,
your mouth in a kiss.

But I can't waste my time
on pink mush
- let the centuries
de-juice it.
Today, prostrate yourselves
at new feet!
I am singing your praises
painted
red-head.

Maybe, when centuries have bleached
my beard,
Maybe all that will remain
of these days,

**terrifying as the points of bayonets,
will be you and me -
throwing myself after you
from town to town.**

**If you are ever sent
somewhere far away
or if you hide yourself
in the hole of night
I will forge kisses on you
with the fiery lips of street lamps
searing the London fog.**

**If you
string out your caravans
in the heat of the desert
where the lions stalk -
I will lay down my cheek
to burn as the Sahara
under the wind-thrashed dust
for you.**

**If you
start to smile at the thought -
'how handsome is the toreador'
in a trice
I'll have hurled my jealousy
at the grandstand
with the murderous eye of the bull.**

**If you
walk out, distracted
onto a bridge
and get it into your mind**

to jump
it will be me, flowing
under that bridge,
the Seine,
calling to you
baring my rotten teeth.

If you,
in a carriage with another,
light up
Sokolniki and Stryelka
with the fire of thoroughbreds
it will be me,
having climbed way up on high,
the Moon,
expectant and naked,
filling you with longing.

Me being strong
if they need me
and order:
'Get yourself killed in the war'
the last thing
clotted
on my bullet-torn lip
will be your name.

Shall I end up crowned?
Or on St Helena?
I who have ridden
the white horses
of Life's storm
am as fit for fetters
as I am to be King of the Universe.

**If I were destined to be Tzar,
on the sunny gold of my coins
your sweet face
I'd command my people:
'Mint!'
And there,
where the world fades into tundra
and the river haggles
with the northern wind,
there I would engrave
on my chains
Lili's name
and frenziedly kiss it
in the darkness of the labour camp.**

**Listen!
You who have forgotten
that the sky is blue,
you who bristle
beast-like,
this might just be
the last Love in the world,
out-dawning all
like a consumptive's flush.**

Then there were all the other women. Preferably very young and very pretty. Considering his enormous size, his manner with women was surprisingly gentle. Even more so if that woman had done him some kindness. Then he was terrified of not showing her enough respect, of hurting her in some way. He never just dropped a woman. He would let her go with the greatest delicacy. He would become most eloquent about it. Ah, the way Mayakovsky treated a woman! His concern with making her life easier - especially if she was working - the presents he'd bring her, the flowers... if women tried to resist him he'd thunder after them with the energy of a steam train - and a tenacious steam train at that! Despite all this, women ultimately chose their husbands or their unremarkable lovers over Mayakovsky - though they didn't generally resist him to begin with. But they had difficulty breathing at Mayakovsky's altitude, he frightened them. He didn't have a movie star's success with the ladies. He entirely lacked that sort of rugged, seductive, insinuating and suggestive approach that women seem to love so much.

It must be said that he wasn't tenacious only where getting a woman he wanted was concerned. His life in general was characterized by obstinacy, courage, and strength of will. All things which are possible only when you are absolutely certain you are right, that your idea of the Truth will inevitably triumph, when you are totally convinced of your own worth... and when you have that mental endurance that Mayakovsky - who lived entirely on his nerves - possessed to a high degree. I won't tell the story here, for example, of the long struggle he had to get his play *Mystery Bouffe* (1918) put on: initially greeted with enthusiasm by Meyerhold and Lunacharsky, it was passed on from one theatre to another and sabotaged in the most petty way by the "art establishment"... and when, in the very end, it was put on in Meyerhold's theatre, got the triumphant success it deserved and ran for ages, Mayakovsky still had to fight to get paid! They told him, straight out, "We should be commended for refusing to pay for this sort of trash." It all ended up in court where it was decided entirely in favour of Mayakovsky.

He never gave up. A defeat for him was only a stage on the road to victory. And yet...

He was often preoccupied, sombre, silent. When he met people he didn't like the look of he'd get very obviously bored and start to be so intensely uncommunicative that people wouldn't stick around... or if that didn't work he'd run over them like a steam roller...

He only liked his "own". He really needed ties - with his country, with his loved ones. Every time he went away from Moscow he nearly died of unhappiness.

He forced himself to travel because he considered it absolutely necessary for his career. Paris was less daunting because I was living there, part of the "family", someone who loves and hates the same things and people as you do, who naturally participates in your own disputes and friendships. He needed to feel trust. He valued loyalty enormously. He demanded it from others and when he gave it himself, it was for life - unto death. That's why people who felt they could rely on him - the nation, those nearest to him - felt such a terrible sense of betrayal when he killed himself.

His behaviour towards his friends was stormy, possessive, closed, violent and, in general - unbearable! He could be really sinister when he wanted to and the most insignificant incident could escalate into a huge drama. He was an extremely demanding friend - he would interpret everything as evidence of neglect or lack of consideration for him... on one of his visits to Paris there was a saga about some soap that cost us three days of brooding silence and tiresome accusations. Mayakovsky was mad about cleanliness and had a morbid fear of picking up any sort of infection. He washed his hands an incredible number of times every day.

When he wasn't at home he had his own special soap that he

carried round in his pocket. While he was in Berlin he had bought a little cake of soap that came in its own little matching tin - Germans love practical items like that. Now he wanted another one - a Parisian one. Obviously I would have to buy it for him since he didn't speak a word of French. But I couldn't find one anywhere - the French are not terribly practical. There were little cakes of soap and little tins but none that were made for each other, none that matched.

"You're doing this deliberately," Mayakovsky insisted. "You just can't be bothered to do anything for me, can you? Obviously it's too much to expect you to do me this one small favour... what? Still no soap? You can't even make the effort to buy me a tiny bit of soap? It's absolutely incredible... very well then, as you please, Madame, I shall have to go out all by myself and search the streets."

And at the end of the third day of sulking: "Goodbye. I shall manage without you." I was weeping with fury. Mayakovsky went out on his own and came back with a beautiful little round aluminium tin. I had great difficulty restraining my glee as I let him wash his hands with a tablet of Gibbs' toothsoap. He had obviously seen this 'soap' in a shop window some time back but instead of buying it had used it to put my friendship to the test.

On the other hand he did once listen to me read an entire manuscript I'd written. That was a real proof of friendship... prose - listening to prose! I really don't think he'd ever done that for anyone before. From then on he often gave me tips about writing techniques and various literary matters - some of which I later found in his work *How Verses Are Made*. Once when we were with some people and I started telling them an anecdote, Mayakovsky suddenly tugged at my sleeve: "Why don't you shut up?" he hissed. "You can use that!" Even quite minor details like this one which I happen to remember: I was telling some people that in certain London cinemas they've got the seats arranged in pairs for the benefit of canoodling couples and that to warn them when the lights are about to go up the girls who sell confectionery start shouting "chocolates! chocolates!" really loudly.

Mayakovsky wanted me to learn to hold my tongue and be economical with my "reserves", to become a professional writer: "Up until now you've been drawing on your 'reserves' to write - if you want to carry on you'll have to keep renewing them. They're not to be squandered."

I also recall what he said to me about worn-out epithets and words that invariably come as a pair... for example "royal bearing" which I had unfortunately used in my book *In Tahiti* when describing the native people of that land. "If you use the word 'bearing' do you have to add 'royal'?" he asked. "It makes me imagine a King with a big beard oozing cabbage soup."

six

Mayakovsky came to Paris for the first time in 1922 when I was away in Berlin. He described the experience in the newspaper *Izvestia* on February 6th 1923:

> **The appearance of a real live Soviet citizen causes a sensation everywhere with an accompaniment of overt surprise, admiration and fascination (at the police station it's just a sensation with no accompaniment). The dominating thing is fascination: I've even had people forming queues in front of my person and keeping me busy answering questions for hours at a time, starting with what Lenin looks like in real life and ending with the very widespread rumour that the women of Saratov have been nationalized!**

If I was in Paris when Mayakovsky visited, he'd install himself in the same little hotel as me. As the only languages he spoke were Russian and Georgian he never let me out of his sight; certain he'd be lost, sold, stitched-up without me! Being thus transformed into a deaf-mute who could only speak what he called "Triolet" made him really furious. He was exasperated by the fact that he couldn't convince everyone that the USSR was the only country worth living in, by not being able to understand what the French were thinking or saying, by not being able to dominate all those around him with his words as he usually did.

> **I hope that foreigners have a good impression of me but it's equally possible that they think I'm an imbecile. Imagine what it's like for the Americans for example: a poet has been invited, they've been told he is a 'genius'. A genius is even better than a**

celebrity. I arrive and point-blank:

   - gif me pliz some tea

Alright, they give me some. I wait a while and then start up again:

   - gif me pliz -

They give me some more and then I say it again and again, with all sorts of tonal modulations:

   - gif me and re-gif me and gif me agen..

I express myself you see and so the charming evening follows its course. Little old men, hale and hearty, listen to me with great respect, no doubt thinking: 'Ah that's the Russians for you - not a word too much. A thinker. Tolstoy. The North.'

Your American thinks while he's working. It would never occur to him to think after six in the evening.

It would never occur to him that I don't actually know a single word of English, that my tongue is spiralling desperately in my head like a corkscrew so eager am I to chat, that my tongue's sticking out like a sewing needle and I'm threading all sorts of 'O's and 'V's on it to no avail since they're completely useless on their own. The American is oblivious of the fact that I am enduring excruciating labour pains culminating in the birth of this wild sentence in Pidgin English:

   'Yes white pliz five double arm strong'

And I imagine that the women, with their kilometres of leg, are simply mesmerised by me: charmed by my accent; transported by my spiritedness; conquered by the profundity of my thoughts. That the men start to shrivel before their eyes and lose all hope, so impossible is it for them to rival me.

But when they've had the tea litany delivered in a charming bass for the hundredth time, the ladies start to shrink back, and the gentlemen retire to corners.

'Would you be good enough to translate this to them,' I yelled at Burliouk, 'That if they could only speak a bit of Russian they'd soon find out how damned sharp my tongue is. It could pin 'em down by their braces without making a mark on their shirts. I could turn over this whole collection of insects with the skewer of my tongue.'

And Burliouk conscientiously translated it thus:
  '- my friend Vladimir is asking if he could have another cup of tea.'

How I Made him Laugh 1926

Mayakovsky's old friend Burliouk, who was thrown out of the Beaux-Arts at the same time as he, was the first person to declare him a poet and a genius - and then insisted he become one so he wouldn't look like a liar.

Burliouk lived in America for quite a while - I'm not sure where, New York or Chicago. Mayakovsky telephoned him when he went there:

"Mayakovsky here."
"Hello Volodya, how are you?"
"I've had a cold in the head for the past ten years, thanks for asking."

(or at least this is how Mayakovsky told me the reunion between the two founders of Russian Futurism went)

Mayakovsky managed to get by using mime and extravagant gestures... if he went to the tailor's he'd solemnly make incredible little sketches, highlighting the defects in his physique and then showing, with dotted lines, the way the suit should correct them. Everywhere we went we encountered a sort of astonishment. This giant played with people like a big dog with children, softly pushing them around and biting without hurting.

On one visit to Paris Mayakovsky got an order from the police station to leave just a few days after he'd arrived. There he was, perfectly docile, doing what all visitors to Paris do: going to the Louvre, to nightclubs, buying himself some shirts and ties... and out of the blue he's being asked to leave! Why? I think they'd got Mayakovsky confused with Esenin: they were both well-known poets and Esenin had left the police in Paris with pretty bad memories for reasons that had nothing to do with politics but with alcohol. Not that Mayakovsky wasn't fond of a drink himself. But anyway, we went to find out what the problem was.

There we were, the two of us, in the police station. I can see us now, wandering round those long corridors that stank of piss, sent from one office to another, me in front, Mayakovsky behind, making a lot of loud clattering with his metal-tipped heels and his cane which he dragged and tapped against walls, doors and chairs.

We finally came to the office of An Important Personage. This was a very irritated gentleman who leapt to his feet behind his desk all the better to shout at us in a furious voice that Monsieur Mayakovsky had better leave Paris within 24 hours. I stammered out a few rather unconvincing things while Mayakovsky kept on interrupting me in a really

able way, constantly asking "What are you saying to him now?... what is he saying?"
- "I'm saying you're hardly dangerous since you don't speak a word of French."
At this, Mayakovsky's face brightened and he looked confidingly at the irritated gentleman and said, in a big, innocent voice:
- "*Jambon!*"
The gentleman stopped shouting, stared at Mayakovsky, then smiled and asked:
- "How long would you like a visa for?"

Mayakovsky finally handed in his passport for the necessary stamps at a counter in the large foyer. The clerk took one look at the passport and said, in Russian, "Oh you're from Bagdadi? I lived there for many years... I had a vineyard..." Both men were delighted with this evidence of how small the world really is.

What with all the emotion of this encounter, Mayakovsky realized too late that he no longer had his cane: someone had pinched it from him right in the middle of a police station!

Talking of being robbed, Mayakovsky didn't stand a chance in Paris. He stood out like a sore thumb. He was so obviously a foreigner - a well-to-do foreigner what's more - that he was instantly targeted by those on the look-out for a victim.

Once he was going to go round the world and came to Paris first. He'd been saving up for ages and had about 25,000 francs with him. One day, God knows why, he took the whole lot out of the bank in cash. Disaster struck the very next day. I'd come round to collect him first thing in the morning. He was sitting in his shirt sleeves eating his breakfast, his "jambon". As we were about to leave, he picked up his jacket which had been hanging over the back of his chair and automatically patted his pockets to make sure everything was there. He suddenly went the colour of cinders - I've never seen anyone lose their colour like that. Someone had stolen all his money. Every centime. His 25,000 francs.

So there he was, at the start of a round-the-world trip which was meant to have lasted a year, with absolutely nothing in his pocket...

Anyone else would have just tried to scrape enough money together to get back to Moscow and returned with his tail between his legs. Not Mayakovsky. He wasn't down about it for long. Even on our way to the police station to report the theft Mayakovsky said - for once forgetting to regulate his steps with mine - "The main thing is not to let this affect our lifestyle. We'll have lunch at *La Grande Chaumiere* and after that I'm going shopping. I'm not going to let life get the better of me."

Whoever robbed Mayakovsky must have been following him from the moment he got the money out of the bank. We found out later that it was a man who had rented the room opposite Mayakovsky's the night before with this express intention. When Mayakovsky went to the bathroom he left his door open and the thief sneaked in, took the money and disappeared from the hotel. A maid and the hotel owner described him to the police and it turned out he was a well known professional thief. This information set us off on a great wild-goose chase - from police station to police station - but we never found either the thief or the money.

However Mayakovsky immediately set about getting money together to make up the sum he'd lost. Someone* gave him quite a considerable sum which he paid back a couple of years later. The rest of it he found where he could. He asked absolutely everybody! And it immediately became a bet. "How much do you reckon so-and-so will give me? 200? I'd say 150 - you can keep the difference if you're right. And him? Nothing? I say 1,000! If he gives me anything you owe me 20 francs." It was 1925. The Exhibition of Decorative Arts was on and there were lots of Soviet Russians in Paris. We started to judge people according to their attitude when they handed over some money, how much they gave or whether they actually gave anything at all. Mayakovsky spurned any friends who had money and refused to give him anything. "Dogs!" he'd say, his gestures, shoulders and face expressing manic disgust... and then he'd persecute them, turning them into a general laughing stock for the rest of their time in Paris. There were also some people who found it extremely funny that this had happened to him. "He's not so smart after all if he gets taken in like that," they kept on saying, smiling from the dizzy heights of their own great wisdom.

On the other hand, if someone gave Mayakovsky more than he reckoned their means and potential generosity would allow, they became an adorable being. Thus Ilya Ehrenburg, whom Mayakovsky had regarded with indifference up until then, conquered him with 50 Belgian francs. Ehrenburg was on his way home from Belgium and only had a little bit of money. Those 50 francs were a constant source of fondness on Mayakovsky's part. "Belgian!" he used to say. "May I draw your attention to the fact that they are Belgian!" and he'd laugh with delight. He started calling Ehrenburg by his first name... and discovered all sorts of new qualities in him.

Even though Mayakovsky had been given the right to remain in Paris that didn't mean the police had lost interest in the case. Wherever we went there were some gentlemen who worked tirelessly at doing exactly the same as us. We must have cost them quite a bit in taxis, food and entertainment.

We ate at the same restaurant every day - *La Grande Chaumière* - because wherever Mayakovsky went he always established a routine after two or three days. We were eating lunch with some friends there once when the two men we'd already spotted came and installed themselves at the table next to ours. One was old and one was young, very French looking, extremely 'correct'... so Mayakovsky started telling us stories and we laughed until we cried under the impassive eyes of our neighbours. Then Mayakovsky launched into the story of a certain billiard game... and that was it! They just couldn't help bursting out with the kind of laughter you can't suppress even if your career - or your life - depends on it.

I saw Mayakovsky for the last time in 1929 - in Paris again. I remember him, sitting on the floor with his note-pad on the bed, writing letters to Moscow. Have you noticed how children always seem to choose the most uncomfortable position for reading or writing? And they can stay in it for hours... Mayakovsky was like that...

Then one day the news came, by telephone, at eight in the morning: Mayakovsky had killed himself the night before, on the 14th April 1930. A bullet through the heart. Death was instantaneous.

These are the opening lines of the letter* they found beside him:

To all of you:

I'm going to die.

Don't blame anyone and please don't gossip - this stiff really hated that.

Mama, sisters, comrades, forgive me. This isn't a good solution (I wouldn't advise anyone else to do it) but I have no other options.

Lili, love me.

Comrade Government, my family are: Lili Brik, Mama, my sisters and Veronika Vitoldovna Polonskaya*. If you can provide a bearable standard of living for them, thank you. Give the verses I've already started to the Briks. They'll sort them out.

As they say - 'The case is closed.'

The love boat
            wrecked
                    on everyday routine.
Life and I are quits,
      and there's no need
           for a list
                of mutual hurts,
                      harms
                          and slights.
Be happy!*

Vladimir Mayakovsky 12th April 1930

TRANSLATOR'S NOTES

page 12

Mayakovsky's father died very suddenly and unexpectedly in 1906 when he pricked his finger with a needle and got blood-poisoning. Mayakovsky developed a fear of needles and some attribute the poet's lifelong obsession with hygiene and washing to this tragedy.

page 13

The Objects Revolt was the original title of *Vladimir Mayakovsky, a Tragedy*.

The yellow blouse - while the modern reader may find nothing shocking about Mayakovsky's famous yellow blouse, so offensive was it to his contemporaries that the police actually banned him from wearing it in 1913 and he had to smuggle it into performances.

page 14

Mayakovsky's drawings - the poet was also an accomplished artist. Many drawings and paintings survive, as well as his graphics. While still a child he had brought money into the fatherless household by selling hand-painted eggs.

page 18

The poem is called *Listen!* (1913)

page 25

Zaoum, also known as transrational or transmental language was an invented language whose relationship to "real" language can be compared with that of Cubism to form. As early as 1910 Khlebnikov had written a poem, *Incantation by Laughter*, which consists entirely of variations on one word,

Smekh (Laughter). Vladimir Markov (1877-1914) made an English version:

> *You who laugh it up and down*
> *Laugh along so laughily*
> *Laugh it off belaughingly*
> *Laughters of the laughing laughniks,*
> *overlaugh the laughathons!*
> *Laughiness of the laughish laughers, counterlaugh*
> *the Laughdom's laughs.*
>
> [extract]

page 26

Lef: The Left Front for Art - an organisation and magazine started by Mayakovsky, Osip Brik and others. Triolet's dates are at odds with other sources here. The consensus is that *Lef* magazine (edited by Mayakovsky and Brik) ceased publication in 1925 and that it was revived in 1927 as *New Lef*. Mayakovsky publicly dissociated himself from both the magazine and the organisation at the end of 1928. Brik then altered its manifesto and changed the name to *Ref* - R for revolutionary, *Lef* having been criticized for its elitism - in 1929 and Mayakovsky rejoined the group until his defection to RAPP (see below) in 1930.

VAPP - Association of Proletarian Writers of the Soviet Union. This organisation was subsequenty absorbed into RAPP (see below)

page 27

RAPP: Russian Association of Proletarian Writers. This organisation became the strongest writers' association, most closely allied to government policy. By 1932 it had taken over every other writers' group.

RAPP favoured Classical Realism and was opposed to the

Futurists. Members of RAPP subjected Mayakovsky to rigorous "re-education" when he joined their ranks - a demeaning experience which some say contributed to his suicide .

a pretty riotous bunch: The Futurists can be compared to the Punk movement of the 1970s. Several leading members (including Mayakovsky) had Anarchist leanings and they flouted authority with flamboyant excess. Their outspoken anti-authoritarianism, Situationist-style 'happenings', rejection of the past, outrageous costumes (eg. spoons in their button-holes, ink drawings on their faces) and predeliction for shouting at, insulting and brawling with their audiences, genuinely shocked and frightened contemporary society.

page 28

Igor Severiannine: *"romantic, pale and a great poseur, he was a leading light in the so-called 'silver period' of Russian literature. His themes were beauties, lace, champagne and a rich, lovely life. His brand of superficial escapism was everything the Revolution (and Mayakovsky) despised."* Dr Paulina Chernilovskaya

page 31

friendship - Elsa's apparently casual attitude to the end of her romantic relationship with Mayakovsky almost certainly belies her suffering when he dropped her in favour of her older sister, Lili Brik. Some commentators believe a sense of betrayal and jealousy prompted her move away from Russia in 1917 and coloured her relationship with Lili for the rest of her life. Lili Brik, incidentally, always dismissed the suggestion that Elsa and Mayakovsky had had a sexual relationship as "unthinkable".

Lili Brik, Triolet's only sibling, was Mayakovsky's lover and muse from 1915 until his death in 1930. She, her husband Osip Brik, and the poet all lived together during this period - an arrangement which scandalised contemporary society and was ignored by later Soviet biographers of the poet.

page 34

The last two lines of Esenin's farewell poem, written in his own blood just before he hanged himself on December 27th 1925.

Esenin was Mayakovsky's closest poetic rival and the latter was outspokenly critical of his melodramatic suicide

page 39

everyday routine - *byt* in Russian. A key concept in understanding Mayakovsky and his work. A kind of paralysing, cosy, bourgeois ordinariness which can also extend to social and literary matters, Mayakovsky despised and feared it. In his suicide note, "the love-boat" is "wrecked on the everyday" [*byt* again]. *About This* was composed during the agonies of a two-month separation imposed on him by Lili Brik in 1923. The reason she gave him was that they were becoming too immersed in *byt*, too cosy with slippers and tea. Interestingly, her letters to Elsa Triolet from this period disclose that the real cause of her disatisfaction with Mayakovsky was his enthusiasm for playing cards!

page 46

a note from Mayakovsky - by now (winter 1916) the poet was usually living with Lili and Osip Brik and one can infer that an argument had taken place. In the same note he told Elsa, "You are the only person in this world I believe I truly love". This has led to some speculation concerning her evident haste to join Mayakovsky.

page 49

hooking up with a foreigner. Elsa was going to Paris to marry a soldier called André Triolet. The marriage was unsuccessful and she later met, and eventually married, the French poet Louis Aragon.

page 50

Lili came by herself - i.e. without Mayakovsky. Their mother was upset about Lili's affair with the poet and her domestic arrangements which she had only just found out about.

page 52

the swelling of hunger - Lili suffered malnutrition due to severe food shortages. Her eyes were widely considered to be particularly beautiful - that they were so badly affected was especially cruel. They did, however, regain their former brilliance on her recovery.

page 56

NEP: New Economic Policy.

page 59

less is the Russian word for forest.

page 61

Gosizdat -the State Publishing House.

page 62

Koulaks - rich Russian peasants.

page 63

Vladimir Ilyitch Lenin - we have not been able to include the very lengthy extract from this poem chosen by Triolet. English translations are available. (See bibliography)

page 64

CCC: Central Control Committee of the Communist Party

page 65

The poem Lenin referred to was *In Re Conferences.*

Stalin only awarded Mayakovsky his recognition (together with its sinister accompanying edict) in 1935, five years after the poet's death, following persistent representations by Lili and Osip Brik.

page 67

Comintern: The Communist International - the Left faction within the Bolshevik party led by Trotsky et al. which was eventually suppressed by Stalin.

page 76

In games and in life - Mayakovsky was a gambler. Shklovsky and other commentators suggest he was playing 'Russian roulette' when he died - he had done so twice before by his own admission. Certainly there was only one bullet in his revolver when Mayakovsky shot himself.

page 91

Someone gave him quite a considerable sum - this was Lili Brik as evidenced by her correspondence with Mayakovsky from this period.

page 92

Mayakovsky's suicide letter is remarkable in several ways. It was written two days before he actually shot himself which has led to much speculation - including the suggestion that he was assasinated by the Chekha (secret police). Then there is the tone, at times incongruously light-hearted: he refers to himself as "this stiff" and makes a pun whereby he mixes the word 'closed' in the line "the case is closed" with a very similar word which means 'peppery'. The note also include lines from verses he was working on at the time ("the love boat/wrecked/on the everyday" for example) adapted to this tragic context.

page 93

Veronika Polonskaya, fondly known as 'Nora', was a young actress with whom Mayakovsky had recently started an affair following his rejection by Tatiana Yakovleva (who married into the French aristocracy).

page 94

Be Happy - the traditional Russian farewell he uses literally means: "Be happy to stay behind."

Ink drawing by Mayakovsky. 1915

SELECTED BIBLIOGRAPHY

Triolet, Elsa, and Brik, Lili, *Correspondance 1921 - 1970*, Gallimard, Paris, 2000.   ISBN 2070729788

Triolet, Elsa, *Écrits Intimes,* Éditions Stock, Paris, 1998. [Triolet's private journals and letters to and from Mayakovsky]

Desanti, Dominique, *Le Couple Ambigu,* Éditions Belfond, Paris, 1994. [A biographical study of Elsa Triolet and Louis Aragon].
ISBN 271443228X

Brown, Edward J., *Mayakovsky, Poet of the Revolution,* Paragon, New York, 1988.   ISBN 1557780021

Mayakovsky, V.V and Brik, Lili, *Love is the Heart of Everything,* correspondence 1915 - 1930, Polygon, Edinburgh, 1986. [Edited and with an exceptionally informative introduction by Bengt Jangfeldt].
ISBN 0948275014

Charters, Anne and Samuel, *I Love*, Andre Deutsch, London, 1979. [A study of the complicated relationship between Mayakovsky and the Briks].   ISBN 0233970703

Mayakovsky, Vladimir, *The Bedbug and selected poetry,* Indiana University Press, 1975. [Edited and with an excellent introduction by Patricia Blake. Translations by Max Hayward and George Reavey]
ISBN 0253211896

Note: English translations of many of Mayakovsky's key poems are available in works by Herbert Marshall, now out of print, as well as in Soviet editions, notably by Progress and Raduga Presses.

HEARING EYE
99 Torriano Avenue London NW5 2RX

Other books available from HEARING EYE include

HAND-PRINTED LETTER PRESS BOOKLETS

The Poems of Sulpicia
Translated by John Heath-Stubbs

Sulpicia is the only woman poet of ancient Rome whose name and work have come down to us. John Heath-Stubbs' excellent translations communicate the feelings of this young patrician woman, speaking with great frankness of her passion for her first lover Cerinthus, to readers two thousand years after her time.

ISBN 1 870841 75 1   £6.00

At Cross Purposes (Paris AD 950)
Translated by Raymond Geuss

There were limits to the hospitality even of a Parisian monastery in the tenth century, as a wandering clerk from east of the Rhine discovers to his cost. The original bi-lingual text (in Old High German and Latin) which records the story of this unusual and amusing encounter is translated by Raymond Geuss, philosopher at the University of Cambridge and poet.

ISBN 1 870841 79 4   £6.00

Encounters
by Dannie Abse

The National Gallery's exhibition 'Encounters' stimulated Dannie Abse to gather here nine literary encounters with foreign poems he has admired. He has departed, sometimes more, sometimes less, from originals by, among others, Mayakovsky, Brecht, Pushkin, Seifert and Amir Gilboa to present new poems that are vivid and successful in English.

ISBN 1 870841 76 X   £6.00

POET FOR POET, Richard McKane, an anthology of new poems and selected translations from Russian and Turkish poets including Akhmatova and Hikmet.
ISBN 1 870841 57 3   £10.99

A.C. Jacobs, COLLECTED POEMS & Selected translations.
ISBN 1 874 320 10 1   £13.99

TERRIFYING ORDEAL, a collection of "rough tough" poems by *Paul Birtill*.
ISBN 1 870841 55 7   £6.00

PARROTS, POETS, PHILOSOPHERS & GOOD ADVICE, Raymond Geuss.
ISBN 1 870841 63 8   £6.00

HOTEL ELISEO, poems by *Harry Eyres*.
ISBN 1 870841 82 4   £6.00

WITNESS TO MAGIC, poems by *Kathleen McPhilemy*.
ISBN 1 870841 131   £6.00

THE FLYING BOSNIAN, poems from limbo, Miroslav Jancic.
ISBN 1 870841 48 4   £6.00

All books are available by post - address for orders as below.

For a full list of HEARING EYE books please write to:

HEARING EYE   99 Torriano Avenue London NW5 2RX